AFRICANITY

Read by MidTerm.
Pg. 3-101

AFRICANITY
THE CULTURAL UNITY OF BLACK AFRICA

JACQUES MAQUET
University of California
Los Angeles

Translated by
JOAN R. RAYFIELD
York University
Toronto

OXFORD UNIVERSITY PRESS
London   Oxford   New York

OXFORD UNIVERSITY PRESS
Oxford   London   Glasgow
New York   Toronto   Melbourne   Wellington
Nairobi   Dar es Salaam   Cape Town
Kuala Lumpur   Singapore   Jakarta   Hong Kong   Tokyo
Delhi   Bombay   Calcutta   Madras   Karachi

printing, last digit: 10 9 8

First published by Oxford University Press, New York, 1972
First issued as an Oxford University Press paperback, 1972

To the memory of Melville J. Herskovits,
who shaped his life on his passionate quest
for the inner understanding of Africa.

CONTENTS

THE CONTENTS OF AFRICANITY

PHOTOGRAPHS

GROUP III

PHOTOGRAPHS BY JACQUES MAQUET

MAPS

MAP DESIGN BY DAVID LINDROTH

AFRICANITY

POLITICAL MAP OF AFRICA SOUTH OF THE SAHARA

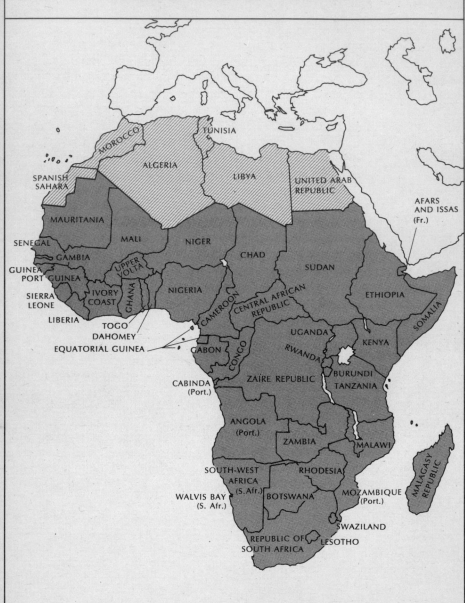

MOROCCO

TUNISIA

ALGERIA

LIBYA

SPANISH
SAHARA

UNITED ARAB
REPUBLIC

AFARS
AND ISSAS
(Fr.)

MAURITANIA

MALI

NIGER

CHAD

SUDAN

SENEGAL

GAMBIA

GUINEA
PORT. GUINEA

UPPER
VOLTA

ETHIOPIA

SIERRA
LEONE

IVORY
COAST

GHANA

NIGERIA

CAMEROON

CENTRAL AFRICAN
REPUBLIC

SOMALIA

LIBERIA

TOGO
DAHOMEY

EQUATORIAL GUINEA

GABON

CONGO

UGANDA

RWANDA

KENYA

CABINDA
(Port.)

ZAÏRE REPUBLIC

BURUNDI
TANZANIA

ANGOLA
(Port.)

ZAMBIA

MALAWI

MALAGASY
REPUBLIC

SOUTH-WEST
AFRICA
(S.Afr.)

RHODESIA

WALVIS BAY
(S. Afr.)

BOTSWANA

MOZAMBIQUE
(Port.)

SWAZILAND

REPUBLIC OF
SOUTH AFRICA

LESOTHO

A CULTURAL CONTINENT

Africa today is a world of great variety. Its diversity cannot be summed up by the smugly stressed opposition between today and yesterday, all too often expressed by the biased terms "town" and "bush." As if pre-colonial Africa had never known city life, as if it had been nothing but bush country, lacking in civilization! In the course of time, Africa has passed through several important stages, besides that of colonization. Its complexity has developed in many dimensions besides that of time. There is the distance between places and also between life-styles, the difference between occupations and also between social functions, the contrast between farmers and herdsmen, and also between rulers and subjects. The African is the Yoruba craftsman and the Tutsi lord, the Nairobi mechanic and the Ibadan professor, the Fulani nomad and the Congolese villager, the hunter of the great forest and the warrior of the high plateaus, the woman trader of Dakar and the factory girl of Bouaké, the Benin sculptor and the Lubumbashi painter. This list of differences within sub-Saharan Africa could be extended indefinitely.

However, the similarities are no less striking. From Conakry to Mogadishu, from Khartoum to Durban, one may perceive a certain common quality. These primary impressions are felt most strongly by foreigners and by Africans who, after some time away from Africa, visit some region of Africa other than that in which they had previously lived. The fact that such circumstances tend to give an impression of unity does not mean that this impression is superficial, but that it requires a certain distance, a comparison, though perhaps an implicit one, with other realities of the same order. To realize that certain styles of life and work are common to people who live in New England or in California one must leave the United States and, more or less consciously, compare them to the French or the Germans.

Life-styles and work-styles are the heart of the matter: human behavior and things made in a social group. It's not the sunshine or the black skin that gives the impression of African unity. It is sunny and hot in all the tropical areas of the world, but that doesn't give one the feeling of being in Africa. There are black sections in many American cities. But Harlem, even on a summer day when it is more humid than Kinshasa in the rainy season, still is not Africa.

Perceiving the Cultural Unity

This unity, strongly though vaguely experienced by the traveler returning to Africa, is a cultural unity. Culture is not interpreted here in its narrow meaning of the appreciation of literature and the fine arts, but in the way it is used in anthropology. It is the totality of knowledge and behavior, ideas and objects, that constitutes the common heritage of a society. We speak of a heritage because as each member of the group grows up he receives this totality that was built up by previous generations and makes it his own; a common heritage, because it is shared by all members of the society. According to the society one belongs to, one wears a loincloth or a jacket, one eats bread or manioc, one marries one woman or several women, one learns to hunt or to farm, one venerates Christ or one's ancestors, one becomes a wage earner or a peasant.

Culture is important then because it makes each of us all that he is, or nearly so. The only things it does not create are those characteristics that depend either on universal human nature or on our own individuality. In our human nature we are like all other men: we are born of a woman, we go through various stages of growth and aging, and we die. In our individual genetic constitution (for example, in having blue eyes because one is the child of a certain man and woman) and in our personal history (for example, in being orphaned very young or in being the victim of a serious accident) we are unique persons, different from every other. Between our universal humanity and our special individuality lies the large part of each of us that is created by the culture handed down to us by our society. The impression of similarity experienced in different parts of Black Africa is based on cultural similarity. It is not because Africans are human beings like all others or because each African is a unique individual that we grasp the common quality of Africa.

The fact of this unity is not based on total, intuitive impressions only. They are confirmed by careful examination of specific cultural phenomena. Thus African sculpture, which evolved in a broad zone extending from the Senegal to the Nile and from Lake Chad to Angola, comprises many styles (one specialist distinguished two hundred); each has its own characteristics. Yet in a museum of "primitive art" it is easy to perceive a certain relationship between African works, a common quality that distinguishes them from works of different origin, since one can pick them out from a collection of traditional pieces from Oceania, America or Asia. It is not because some particular feature is found in all African sculptures, and only in them, but because a certain cluster of characteristics gives African art its own special look.

It is the same with African languages; there are many of them. According to the criteria chosen, we may count from seven hundred to fifteen hundred. One language family, the Niger-Congo, extends over a large area, almost the whole of that part of the continent to the south of a line drawn from Dakar to Mombasa. Yet despite this vast expanse and great diversity the Niger-Congo languages have enough common features to justify their classification as a single family.*

* Joseph H. Greenberg, *Languages of Africa*. Mouton & Co., The Hague, 1966.

Similar conclusions may be drawn from areas of culture other than art and language. Social institutions (such as marriage, the family and political organizations), belief systems and world views also display common qualities throughout sub-Saharan Africa.

Several books have indeed been written to set forth and explain the special quality of Black Africa.*

In the sphere of action, too, the unity of Africa has been recognized. Intellectually, this means the affirmation of negritude; politically, it means the Pan-African movement.

Claiming One's Negritude

The concept of negritude must be understood in the light of the circumstances in which it developed in black intellectual circles in Paris about 1935. At this time, when colonization by conquest was over, when Europe was quietly establishing itself in Africa, to stay there indefinitely, black students had doubts about their own cultures. The colonial expatriates were bringing "Western civilization" to Africa. However, it was sifted and censored for African consumption, for "not everything European is suitable for these Negroes, who are just grown-up children," and "so that they will respect the Whites they had better not see certain things." In the eyes of the colonists, European civilization—called "civilization" without qualification—was being transplanted into a sort of cultural desert. European law encountered not another legal system but barbarous customs, monogamous marriage was substituted not for another form of marriage but

* The most important ones include: Maurice Delafosse, *L'Âme nègre*. Payot, Paris, 1927; Léo Frobénius, *Histoire de la civilisation africaine*. Gallimard, Paris, 1952 (originally published in German, 1933); Cheick Anta Diop, *The Cultural Unity of Negro Africa*. Présence africaine, Paris, 1962 (originally published in French, 1959); Janheinz Jahn, *Muntu: An Outline of the New African Culture*. Grove Press, New York, 1961 (originally published in German, 1958); Melville J. Herskovits, *The Human Factor in Changing Africa*. Knopf, New York, 1962; Paul Bohannan, *Africa and Africans*. Natural History Press, New York, 1964; Basil Davidson, *The African Genius. An Introduction to African and Cultural History*. Little, Brown, Boston, 1969.

for immoral concubinage, Christian religions were opposed not to other religions but to absurd superstitions.

The material power the Whites displayed in Africa and the strong psychological pressure exercised by colonial administrations and missionaries deeply shook the views of certain Africans concerning their social heritage. They judged it from the European point of view, and, as it was their own, they were ashamed of it. To heal this split, many intellectuals turned to assimilation and aimed at becoming "Black Europeans." But still, they were black, and their black skins made a mockery on the social level of the assimilation that had been fully achieved on the cultural level. The black doctor was treated with condescending familiarity by the white shopkeeper.

Negritude is a concept of synthesis. But above all it is a total attitude of response to a situation. Aimé Césaire, who, with Léopold Sédar Senghor, Léon Damas and a few other young intellectuals, coined the term "negritude," defined it as "the consciousness of being black, the simple recognition of a fact, implying acceptance of and responsibility for one's destiny as a black man, one's history and one's culture." And Senghor wrote: "It is first a negation as I have said, more precisely the affirmation of a negation. It is the necessary moment of a historical movement: the refusal to assimilate, to lose oneself in the Other. But because this is a historical movement, it is by the same token a dialectical one. Refusal of the Other is affirmation of the Self." This affirmation of the self in the face of Western civilization led these black intellectuals living in Europe to take cognizance of an African civilization over and above the differences between their various social heritages. Thus the concept of negritude transcends tribal and national particularities. It is, in Senghor's words, "the cultural heritage, the values and above all the spirit of black African civilization."*

Liberating All Africa

Thus negritude justified the refusal of the dependence relationship the colonists sought to establish, for it gave a foundation to

* Lilyan Kesteloot, *Les Écrivains noirs de langue française: naissance d'une littérature*. Institut de sociologie, Brussels, 1963, pp. 110, 112-14.

the struggle to win back African identity. It enabled all black
people to feel that their solidarity was not only negative—the
struggle against colonialism—but positive—the affirmation of
the right to live within a common civilization. As an ideological
weapon, negritude encountered a movement that had a different
origin—Pan-Africanism. This movement arose at the beginning
of this century among English-speaking Blacks, especially those
of the United States and the British West Indies. The first Pan-
African conference was organized in London in 1900 by a Trini-
dad lawyer, Henry S. Williams. After World War I it was
expanded on the initiative of George Padmore and W. E. B.
Dubois. In their view, the struggle of one people for its national
independence strengthened the struggles of all the others and
was strengthened by them: colonial rule must be fought by
united action, not piecemeal. Negritude, the intellectual stand
and Pan-Africanism, the political stand converged in that they
both affirmed, first, that all Africans had a common civilization
and, second, that all Africans must fight together.*

The total intuition of the reality of African life, the analysis
of artifacts and institutions, the claims of negritude, the political
action of Pan-Africanism converge on the same point: sub-
Saharan Africa is culturally a unity. This cultural unity is
Africanity. It is the special African configuration of various
features that may be found separately elsewhere. All human
faces are made up of the same elements: nose, eyes, mouth, etc.;
one or another of these elements may be identical in form in
several faces, but the combination of these features forms one
unique face. Africanity is this unique cultural face that Africa
presents to the world.

At the beginning of this book I spoke of the cultural multiplicity of Africa. How can this be reconciled with the affirmation
of unity denoted by Africanity?

It is true that each society has its own heritage, its *culture*.
To avoid confusion, let us continue to use this term in its exact
sense: the totality of ways of living, working and thinking and
the totality of what results from these activities (institutions,

* Philippe Decraene, *Le Panafricanisme*. Presses Universitaires de France,
  Paris, 1959.

artifacts, philosophies, etc.) as they are constituted in a given society. Each society has built up a culture, each culture is based on a society.

There are many traditional societies in Africa. A society is a group of men and women, living and working together, who by their complementary activities provide at the same time for the survival of the group and the satisfaction of the material and psychological needs of each individual. The whole life of each member is normally lived within his society. Members of a society are aware of their membership: they call themselves by a common name, and this sets up clear boundaries between groups. Bearing its own name, each society is easily distinguishable by the anthropologist. Thus one anthropologist George P. Murdock, in a well-known book lists and describes almost 850 traditional African societies,* which means 850 different cultures.

But these actual cultures may be gathered together into a few large groups: civilizations. Each civilization comprises the common qualities of a certain number of actual cultures, which are essentially similar to each other. I have attempted elsewhere to group African cultures into six major civilizations.† These are: the civilization of the bow, that of the hunters of the equatorial forest and the savannas of southern Africa; the civilization of the clearings, that of the forest farmers; the civilization of the granaries, that of the agriculturists who have built the great chiefdoms and kingdoms of the savanna belt extending across Africa to the south of the equatorial forest belt; the civilization of the spear, that of the warrior herdsmen of the vast area of the high plateaus of East Africa; the civilizations of the cities, that of the craftsmen, the traders and the rulers of the steppes and dry savanna on the edge of the Sahara; and finally the civilization of steel or industry, that of the workers, clerks and entrepreneurs living throughout Africa, wherever factories and new towns are found.

* George Peter Murdock, *Africa: Its Peoples and Their Culture History.* McGraw-Hill, New York, 1959.
† Jacques Maquet, *Civilizations of Black Africa.* Oxford University Press, New York, 1972 (originally published in French, 1962).

These civilizations are cultural units, but, unlike cultures, they are not realities of which their members are directly aware. A member of the Nkole society knows that he speaks the Nkole language, lives in the Nkole style and must abide by the Nkole customs; but he is not conscious of belonging to a civilization of warrior herdsmen that extends "in East Africa from the marshy plains of the White Nile, home of the Nuer, the Dinka and the Shilluk, near the tenth parallel north, to the hills of Natal about the thirtieth parallel south, where the Zulu live." Similarly, a Norwegian villager is not directly aware of belonging to the Scandinavian civilization. Why? The term "civilization" as it is used here is a conceptual tool that enables the anthropologist to analyze and understand facts. It is an interpretation, with an objective basis, of course, but it must be read into the facts. It, too, is direct experience, but the experience of the observer, not the participant. A person who is somewhat familiar with the villages of the Zaïre savanna, the cities of the Sudan and the hamlets of the high plateaus of East Africa feels intuitively that they belong to three civilizations, but a person who knows only his own society and the neighboring ones is more aware of differences than resemblances.

Africanity is also a conceptual tool that enables us to grasp what the various African civilizations have in common. It is very close to the concept of negritude but different in its orientation. While the essential function of negritude is to affirm a previously alienated cultural personality, Africanity aims at understanding and analysis.

Cultures, civilizations and Africanity represent three levels of generalization, but these concepts express, each in its own way, the richness of the traditions of Black Africa. They are not mutually exclusive, they are complementary.

This cultural unity of Africa is a fact. On what is it based? Why do we find this cultural community throughout sub-Saharan Africa?

Having a Black Skin
Does not the question supply the answer? We say Black Africa. Is it not because they have been developed by men and women

of the black race that the various African cultures display a profound unity?

Though racism—belief in the superiority of one race—is a social phenomenon, race is a purely biological concept. In classical physical anthropology, this term denotes human groups that have in common certain hereditary physical characteristics, that is, characteristics that cannot be acquired by an individual during his lifetime. A racial group is defined by an assemblage of physical features that are in some way measurable: skin color, hair type and stature and the shape of the head, face, nose and eyes. For the last few decades, the proportion of the various blood groups in a population has also been taken into consideration. The variations in each of these features—especially the last—do not always coincide, and this gives a certain vagueness to racial classifications. For a very long time the terms "race" and "tribe" were used interchangeably in describing traditional African groups. To justify this usage, there would have to be complete parallelism between the cultural and the genetic heritage of a group. We shall now consider this problem.

This parallelism between cultural and biological features is at the heart of controversies over racism, because it is the basis on which racists claim that their position is scientifically established. According to the racists, the visible physical differences between the races are paralleled by profound mental differences, both intellectual and emotional, so that individuals of certain races are not capable of achieving the same intellectual development as those of other races and have a kind of character that makes them unable to command and predisposes them to obey. Such is the "scientific" basis of the doctrine of the inequality of races.

The crimes this doctrine has attempted to justify—the fifteen or twenty million Africans sold as slaves in three centuries, the six million Jews exterminated by the Germans in six years—are such that its "scientific basis" has been cautiously, assiduously and earnestly examined by many research teams. The results obtained, then, are especially reliable. So that they should be disseminated as widely as possible, UNESCO in 1951 fortunately took the initiative, unusual in science, of calling together a group of anthropologists and geneticists and asking them to prepare a common declaration setting forth what can be scientifically stated on this question. This precise and cautious text concludes that "in the present state of knowledge, there is no justification for the belief that human groups differ in natural aptitudes, either intellectual or emotional," and that "certain biological variations may be as great or greater within the same race than between one race and another."*

Thus culture and race are independent variables. It is not because one belongs to a certain race that one speaks a certain language or practices agriculture. Africans did not create Africanity because they are black. Strangely enough, this second proposition is less easily accepted than the first. And yet each is as ascertainable as the other. Actually, "the scientific data at present available do not support the theory according to which hereditary genetic differences are a primary factor in determining the differences between cultures and their expression in various populations or ethnic groups." This statement, also from the UNESCO declaration, applies as much to Africanity as to specific cultures.

Being a Member of a Black Race

Furthermore, in order to explain the cultural unity of Africa by racial factors, there would have to be a significant degree of racial homogeneity throughout Africa. Now, the Blacks, who constitute one of the three major groups into which the human species is divided (classical anthropology calls these the three main stocks), must be classified into various groups with very different racial characteristics. Within the Negroid stock Henri-V. Vallois distinguishes four races in sub-Saharan Africa: The Khoisan race (at present a few tens of thousands of Bushmen and Hottentots driven back into the arid areas of southern Africa), the Negrito race (the Pygmies of the equatorial forest, famous for their small stature), the Ethiopian, or rather, Ethiopoid race (which occupies the East Horn; although these people

* Georghi F. Debetz, "Biology Looks at Race." UNESCO *Courier*, April 1965, pp. 4-11.

display characteristics intermediate between those of the Whites and those of the Black Africans, they are apparently not the result of interbreeding but form a distinct race) and the Black African race (by far the most important; it dominates all of sub-Saharan Africa west of the East Horn).

Even if one arbitrarily limited the racial "basis" of Africanity to the Black African race, one would not get a homogeneous substratum. Actually, Vallois has distinguished subraces as displaying such varied physical characteristics that, on the basis of anthropometric measurements, he can "provisionally" identify five in Africa. These are: the Sudanese subrace (in the savanna belt that extends between the equatorial forest and the Sahara, from Senegal to Kordofan), the Guinean subrace (in the forest belt that follows the coast from Guinea to Cameroon), the Congolese subrace (in the equatorial forest and the savanna belt to the south of it), the Nilotic subrace (in the marshes and grasslands of the Nile, from Khartoum to Lake Victoria) and the Zambezian subrace (in the eastern half of the continent, from the Great Lakes to the southern tip).*

A black "race" is an illusion if one means by it a homogeneous group with common anatomical and physiological characteristics. Actually, it is a group of races comprising, in Africa, four races and several subraces. Of course this classification is open to question, but it is certain that one can find among the Blacks a number of groups, each characterized by a cluster of hereditary features. Finally, the Blacks have nothing more in common than a more or less dark skin and kinky hair. A limited basis to account for the cultural unity of Africa! Especially since there are Blacks outside Africa: in Asia there are the Black peoples of India and in Oceania the Negrito and Melanesian peoples.

Africanity, then, is not based on the community of a common race. And negritude? Of course the term itself has racial overtones. Also Senghor's opposition of the Black African mind, "intuitive by participation," to the classic European mind, "analytic by utilization," suggests a constitutional hereditary differ-

* Henri-V. Vallois, *Les Races humaines*, Presses Universitaires de France, Paris, 1944.

ence; Jean-Paul Sartre's definition of negritude, approved by Senghor, is similar: "a certain affective attitude to the world."* Finally, the inclusion of Black American communities in the Black world as seen by Alioune Diop's journal *Présence Africaine* seems to give primacy to racial origin.

Negritude, however, is not basically a racial concept. If it were, Senghor and Césaire would have clearly said so. But, since it is a response to white racism, it must inevitably include certain racial overtones. As Fanon wrote, "It is the white man who creates the Negro."† The colonist did not distinguish between race and culture: for him, to be black and to be pagan was the same thing; the inference was the same state of inferiority to two other synonyms: white and civilized. The reaction was to assume responsibility for one's black skin together with ancestor worship. Being an instrument of liberation, negritude had to affirm what the white man denied; it would have been less effective if it had not answered the challenge in the same terms. But nothing justifies the belief that the inventors and wielders of this weapon wanted to give a fundamentally racial basis to the cultural specificity of Africa.

From our own viewpoint of description and analysis, the concept of Africanity enables us to attain greater precision than would be possible if we were constrained by the demands of action.

Being African and White

By limiting the domain of Africanity to the area south of the Sahara, do we not reintroduce the concept of race, since the peoples of the Maghreb are of white stock?

---

* Léopold Sédar Senghor, "De la négritude. Psychologie du Négro-Africain." *Diogène*, N. 37, pp. 9, 11, Gallimard, Paris, 1962. See "The Psychology of the African Negro." *Negritude: Essays and Studies*, ed. Albert Berrian and Richard Long, Hampton Institute Press, Hampton, Va., 1967, pp. 48-55.

† Frantz Fanon, *A Dying Colonialism*. Penguin Books, Harmondsworth, 1970 (originally published in French, 1959). (Quoted by Kesteloot, 1963:116.)

It cannot be denied that the separation of these two worlds is definite and rests on well-established academic traditions. There are specialists in Islamic civilizations who do in fact study the societies and cultures of Africa north of the Sahara. In their view, the Maghreb is attached to Arabic Islam and, through it, to the Islamic world that extends from Rabat to Djakarta.

Certainly, on the cultural level, the societies north and south of the great desert have had more contacts throughout their history than was thought a few decades ago. A network of regularly used caravan trails connected the Mediterranean coast with the Niger and Lake Chad. From the eleventh century, Islam had adherents in the kingdom of Ghana and the other city-states that arose in the Sudan region. The Nile Valley too was a link between Egypt and the East Horn, especially through the Cushite kingdoms of Nepata and Meroë (700 B.C. to A.D. 400) and later through Axum.

However, these exchanges between the peoples living on the borders of the Sahara were not sufficiently intense or numerous to create a cultural unity. This was even more true of the rest of Africa, separated as it was by the great equatorial forest from the areas immediately to the south of the Sahara. Of course the Maghreb civilization belongs to the continent of Africa, but it does not seem to me to belong to Africanity. Not so much because it is a literate civilization, while the others are without writing, but mostly because it did not participate in that slow process of development shared by the societies south of the Sahara and west of the Abyssinian bloc.

The two Africas, one each side of the Sahara, are distinct on cultural grounds, not because the inhabitants of one are classified with the white race and of other with the black.

THE SOURCES OF AFRICANITY

If Africanity is not based on common race, how is it to be explained? Must we have recourse to a sort of Platonic idea, an immutable essence, an African soul or spirit? No, the explanation is less mysterious and more complex. Like every broad cultural synthesis, Africanity is based on a similar experience of the world shared by various societies and on the dissemination of several culture traits among these societies. Two mechanisms are operating: the development of similar ways of adapting to the natural environment and the diffusion of culture traits. These two mechanisms, each reinforcing the other, combine to create a common culture.

The primary and closest contact between an African society and its environment is not contemplation but action. And it is a very specifically oriented action: man must obtain from nature what is necessary for the group's survival. It is this that ensures the members of the society will be fed. This is why the production of material goods is the most important activity of all societies. It depends on two elements: the type of environment (forest, grassy savanna, dry steppe, etc.) and the techniques available to a society (grassy savanna has a completely different meaning depending upon whether one possesses bow and arrows, hoe, plow, tractor, chemical fertilizer or cattle).

Sub-Saharan Africa comprises a variety of habitats: the great, always green equatorial forest with its giant trees, their roots partly exposed above the moist, often marshy ground, its luxuriant and hard-to-penetrate vegetation; the dry forest of deciduous trees; the grassy highland savannas with patches of canopy forest along the rivers; the dry wooded savanna; the arid steppes, like the Sahel belt, on the edge of the Sahara, Kalahari and Namib deserts.

Tilling the Land

From the point of view of subsistence, these various habitats have in common the fact that they are not very favorable to agriculture. The luxuriant vegetation of the great rain forest does not indicate that the soil is fertile. Its soils are chemically poor, and the layer of humus is so thin that clearing reveals layers of sand on which even the forest can barely grow again after man has cultivated it. The heavy rains that fall all the year round leach the soil, cause erosion as they drain off and, finally, produce laterization of the soil.* The dry zones seem to be no more fertile. There are only a few areas that favor agriculture: river deltas and valley bottoms intersecting the high plateaus.

To exploit this difficult habitat, the African tool is the hoe, and the methods most commonly used are long fallowing, rotation of crops and slash-and-burn. These techniques are crude, but the nature of the soil admits of no other. The introduction of the plow by European agronomists has often met with failure: its blade cuts too deeply into the earth, bares sterile strata and facilitates erosion. Burning consists in setting fire, toward the end of the dry season, to the dead or wild vegetation left in the fields after the harvest; thus the earth is enriched by ashes before the sowing. This practice, often criticized by foreign experts, is one of the few means of fertilization possible where there is no manure because of the absence of large domestic

* Pierre Gourou, *The Tropical World: Its Social and Economic Conditions and Its Future Status*. Longmans, London, 1958 (originally published in French, 1948).

animals. In the dense forest, this method permits the clearing of
land after the large trees have been felled.

Even with annual burning, the same field cannot be cultivated
over a long period. Long fallowing may be necessary, sometimes
for twenty years after two or three harvests. This gives rise to a
shifting agriculture. When all the fields surrounding a village
are in fallow it is better to avoid long journeys between home
and work by moving the village and rebuilding it in the middle
of the land in current use.

Rotation of crops is another method of preserving the fertility
of the soil. In the course of the same season several different
crops are planted or sown. Thus among the Rega (who live at
the edge of the equatorial forest in Zaïre) rice is first sown
broadcast. When it begins to grow, manioc shoots are planted at
intervals and, a few weeks later, banana roots.

The cultivated plants that form the basic diet of African societies are cereals (sorghum, eleusine, maize) and pulses (peas,
haricots, beans), most important in the savannas; root crops
(manioc, yams, sweet potatoes), in the equatorial and Atlantic
forests; and bananas, especially common in the humid regions
and the high plateaus of the east.

Hunting

Africans live mostly on farm products. But what about the
civilizations of hunters and herdsmen?

Hunting and gathering imply living off nature without modi-
fying it. This was the technique used by humanity for longer
than ninety-nine per cent of its existence: from its origins to
what has been called the Neolithic Revolution, the invention of
agriculture and the domestication of animals. The African continent was probably the scene of two events of prime importance.
Modern man (Homo sapiens) is the descendant of other species
now extinct but of which we possess a few skeletal remains.
With the help of these fragments, paleontologists have reconstructed the major anatomical forms that constitute the ancestry
of Homo sapiens. Which of the forms in this sequence may be
regarded as representing the transition from animal to man? The
criterion adopted by most prehistorians is the manufacture of

tools. Of course these are very crude tools, such as stone hand axes. It is in Africa, in the Olduvai Valley in Tanzania, that Louis Leakey and his wife discovered stone tools in association with a fossil skull that Leakey called *Homo habilis*. This skull, which has been dated as 1,850,000 years old, is thought to be that of the oldest known toolmaker, a million years earlier than the Java man, whom some consider to be the oldest known ancestor of modern man. Thus in the present state of our knowledge it is highly probable that Africa is the cradle of humanity.

Between this long-distant period and the discovery of agriculture, which is thought to have occurred about ten thousand years ago, man lived by hunting and gathering. So the Neolithic Revolution occurred only yesterday, since these ten thousand years represent only one-half of one per cent of the time that has elapsed since the man of Tanzania made his crude stone tools. (This percentage is in no way precise, but it helps us visualize the ratio between the two spans of time.) During this seemingly interminable first stage of human history, hunting techniques improved slowly; this improvement may be traced in Africa as in other parts of the world: chipping stones to produce a sharper cutting edge or point, polishing to make tools more effective; learning to control fire; inventing new weapons (spears, darts and bows and arrows).

Although Africa was probably the only place man emerged, it is not the only place the agricultural and pastoral revolution occurred. It has recently been recognized that Africa was probably one of the four centers in which agriculture was independently developed. About ten thousand years ago, over a period of some three or four thousand years, the most important cultural change that humanity has known up to the Industrial Revolution occurred in Southeast Asia, Central America, Western Asia and West Africa. We know that agriculture existed south of the Sahara about seven thousand years ago. It was probably introduced from two centers: the fertile crescent of Western Asia (through Egypt) and the bend of the Niger.* Gradually agriculture replaced hunting and gathering as the

* Murdock, op. cit., pp. 64 ff.

main subsistence technique. At the time the Industrial Revolution brought the third cultural era of human history to Africa, hunting became marginal. Societies belonging to the civilization of the bow are few and now comprise only a few tens of thousands of individuals in the savannas and dry steppes of Southern Africa and less than two hundred thousand spread through the equatorial forest. These hunters exchange part of what they obtain in the forest and the savanna for farm products grown by neighboring groups of cultivators. On the other hand, wherever the environment allows, some members of the group, whether they live in a peasant village, a herding camp or a city of artisans, hunt to supplement their food supply.

Herding

Unlike the civilization of the bow, the civilization of the spear of the warrior herdsmen of East Africa is far from being on the road to extinction. Cattle are the prime social value; all interests, desires and dreams converge upon them; on them rest prestige, fame and power; around them are organized institutions, rituals and ceremonies. However the basic diet of these pastoralists consists of agricultural products. Certainly some groups, such as the Hima of the Great Lakes, can live exclusively on the products of their herds during the periods they nomadize. Certainly in mixed societies composed of a lower class of peasants and a ruling class of pastoralists, as in Ankole or Rwanda, superior status is attached to dairy produce and to meat, the consumption of which is a sign of social rank. But these cases, and others of the same order that might be mentioned, remain exceptional: the East African pastoral societies have in their daily diet more agricultural than pastoral products.

Herding is not confined to the civilization of the spear. But elsewhere it is not the center of a complex system of beliefs, emotions and social relationships. It has a more directly utilitarian value. Most commonly it is part of a mixed farming system and contributes to a peasant-type subsistence. More rarely, as for the nomadic Fulani, it constitutes the basic means of production.

Living on Little

The basis of any society—the system of productive techniques—is essentially the same throughout Africa. The subsistence farmer obtains from a poor soil, with simple but well-adapted tools, a yield that is of necessity low, that is, which provides a very small surplus above what the producer must consume. To the main reason for this low productivity—the poor quality of the soils—must be added the fact that large areas, the rain forest, for example, are very unhealthy for both men and animals. The many endemic tropical diseases lower the capacity for work; sleeping sickness precludes cattle-raising in many savanna areas.

Hunting is a difficult and dangerous activity with low nutritional returns. Stock-raising, too, has a very limited yield. The animals have as their food only what the natural habitat supplies. This means that almost everywhere during a long dry season the cattle, without green pasture and sufficient water, waste away and stop giving milk. Nowhere is meat a daily food.

As we have said elsewhere, the life experiences of the hunter, the forest cultivator, the savanna agriculturalist and the pastoralist are different. However they have this in common: obtaining the necessities of life is not easy and requires constant effort; survival is always unsure, for the margin is narrow, and every year there is a critical period of scarcity. In this narrow but fundamental aspect, the African's existential experience is everywhere the same.

Expanding the Existential Experience

The consequences of this similarity are not restricted to the level of acquisition or production of subsistence commodities; they also influence broad aspects of culture: man's vision and explanation of the universe and his conception of the gods and of the relationships he can and must maintain with the invisible world. This is not a mysterious determinism but the normal operation of human mental processes. Depending upon our experience and needs, by generalization and projection, we build our conception of the world. Being continuous with our direct perception of reality, this conception is confirmed by what we see, and, when it takes into account what we expect of life, it answers our psychological requirements. Thus a group in which all the adult members must spend the greater part of their energy wresting enough food for their needs from their environment will have a different view of nature from that of a group in which a few of the members can produce plenty of food for all. People whose harvest is every year at the mercy of a dry spell need a different kind of psychological security from that needed by people who fear a drop in the stock market. A cattle epidemic is a very different experience according to the means a society has to combat it; if the group possesses the means to check an epidemic through veterinary science, it will have a more optimistic point of view than if it has no means at its disposal. In the latter case it would be psychologically unbearable to feel oneself helpless, to submit without taking action, thus one will attempt to do something, nonetheless, about the cattle disease, by creating an invisible world in which man can influence events by magical powers or through the mediation of gods or spirits.

Areas other than those of mental representations are influenced, and very directly, by a society's techniques of acquisition and production: these are economic, familial and political. Here it is more a matter of negative determinism (certain institutions are precluded by certain technical levels) and of a determinism of suitability (certain types of social organization fit particularly well with certain techniques).

If the productivity of a type of subsistence is low, that is, if a group, in order to feed itself, has to use a large area of land— which is the case for hunting and gathering and also for forest cultivation—the society cannot consist of a large number of people living in dense, stable groups. A city of hunters is an impossibility. Similarly, if a society does not produce a surplus, that is, if each unit of production consumes all it produces, that society cannot have a state level of political organization, since no section of the group can devote itself entirely to government. In such a society specialization of labor can be only rudimentary, for since each unit produces only enough for its own subsistence, no artisan can forgo cultivating his own field. To place oneself in relationship to one's fellow men as the descendant of a line of ancestors is a way of organizing human relationships that is perfectly appropriate where communities are small and lack state structure.

Thus the basis of this family of civilizations that we call Africanity gradually reveals its solidity. The cultural unity of Africa does not rest on a mysterious African soul, an ideal essence or a certain way of feeling, but on a material base: the similarity of acquisition and production and their low yield. This is not its only basis, for, out of this develop cultures that, though different, still reflect it.

This is only the first stage of our attempt to understand Africa. For these subsistence techniques are not peculiar to Africa. Elsewhere in the world agricultural societies have lived on poor land, getting their food mostly from cultivation or occasionally from herding and gathering. Yet this does not make them "African."

Moving about

Almost every African population has come from "elsewhere." Oral traditions handed down from generation to generation preserve the memory of these migrations. When certain indicators make it possible to check these tales of origin, their historical nature is usually confirmed. These indicators are sometimes facts attested by documents of the type normally used by historians (archives and monuments) and often are linguistic phenomena. Indeed their permanence enables us to discover very ancient contacts between populations.

A well-known, because recent, case shows that population movements can take place in a relatively short time and over great distances. In the nineteenth century, between 1850 and 1890, in less than forty years a group of Sumbwa (in present-day Tanzania) established a rather large kingdom, Garenganze, in the Katanga region (now in Zaïre) more than six hundred miles from their point of origin. Their chief, who took the royal name of Msiri, organized his state starting from a capital, Bunkeya, a large village of from twelve to fifteen thousand inhabitants. He naturally introduced customs from his home country, in particular symbolic insignia of power (certain shells), ritual, wood-carving techniques and a system of rule through tributary chiefdoms.

Throughout African history events of this kind seem to have been very frequent. From the point of view of Africanity they are very important, for they brought into contact different cultures that borrowed from each other. Thus a common African inheritance was gradually built up.

Migrating

More important in this connection were the great migrations of whole populations. Their history is largely conjectural. But although points of origin and itineraries are still often hypothetical, it is certain that slow migrations occurred. Those of the Bantu-speaking peoples indicate their magnitude.

Today, with a few exceptions, all the languages spoken south of a line starting at Douala and going east along the northern boundary of the equatorial forest to the Indian Ocean at Mombasa, belong to the Bantu family. According to linguists, it seems highly probable that all these languages have a common origin and that this common origin is not very far back in time, about three thousand years ago. The region where this mother language was spoken can be determined by linguistic criteria. It is the Bauchi plateau in present-day Nigeria. To spread from this center into the present territory of the Bantu languages the savanna cultivators must have penetrated the equatorial forest or gone around it. Here the botanists come in. They point out that crops of the Sudanese savanna, millet and rice, were not suitable for the rain forest; that consequently the Bantu could not penetrate the equatorial zone—up to that time inhabited only by hunters and gatherers—until they had acquired root crops (yams and taro) and bananas. Now, it is unlikely that these plants, which originated in Southeast Asia and spread to Africa by way of the Indian Ocean coast, could have reached the edge of the forest in present-day Cameroon before the beginning of the Christian era. Perhaps the Bantus went around the forest, skirting its eastern edge and turning south by way of the high plateaus of the Great Lakes region, a region suitable for population movements. They may also have followed the Atlantic coastline. It seems likely that there are secondary centers of the Bantu-speaking peoples' migrations in the Lake Kisale area (in northern Katanga in present-day Zaïre) and in the Kinshasa region.* These Bantu peoples were acquainted with iron working and introduced it throughout the whole of Southern Africa. This meant the diffusion of the hoe, the peasants' essential tool.

Diffusing

There are many unanswered questions, but the knowledge we have acquired is enough to throw light on one of the development processes of Africanity. Starting from a single origin, north of the equatorial forest, two important cultural realities, a language and a technique, spread over half a continent in a relatively short time. Whether the actual populations all came from this source (which is unlikely, in view of the diversity of present-day physical types), or whether the Bantu-speaking immigrants met other groups who adopted their cultural contributions, does not much matter. What matters is the broad area of diffusion of these contributions. Is it surprising that we find definite culture traits—certain beliefs, art forms, etc.—common to the societies dwelling in this half-continent? These recurrences would be difficult to explain by only the similarity of subsistence techniques. For although such techniques exclude certain institutions, certain conceptions, certain styles, they usually allow for more than one compatible cultural form. These recurrences become understandable when we know that the Bantu migrations stirred up a cultural mixing continent-wide in extent.

Another example of large population movements is found in the highland area between the Great Lakes of East Africa: Lakes Albert, Edward, Kivu, Tanganyika and Victoria, in the present-

* Murdock, op. cit., pp. 271-74.

day states of Uganda, Rwanda and Burundi. We can often still distinguish in the present population the descendants of different waves of invaders. And all of Black Africa meets here. First the hunters. Probably the earliest inhabitants of the territory, they are now very few in number, carrying on the way of life of their ancestors in the high forest that covers the chain of mountains between the Nile and Congo basins. In spite of interbreeding most of these hunting peoples retain their distinctive Negrito racial characteristics.

Borrowing

The history of these migrations may be reconstructed, hypothetically, as follows. Pastoralists of the Ethiopoid racial type came from the northeast and penetrated the area in several waves. The first invaders may have come a long time ago, perhaps about 1000 B.C., while the latest (for example, the Tutsi of Rwanda) probably came about A.D. 1200 and 1300. Concurrently, at the beginning of our era, a number of the Bantu-speaking peasants we have just mentioned came into the region from the west and northwest. As in other cases, they brought their language, agriculture and iron. Also, as in other cases, they assimilated culturally and racially the pastoral peoples who were already in the area. Actually, only the last wave of Ethiopoid invaders—the Chwezi, the Tutsi and the Hima—to some degree retained their cultural identity (they speak a Bantu language but do not practice agriculture) as well as their racial identity.

The Chwezi set up a kingdom called Kitara. Recent excavations have revealed terracing around a system of trenches of which the elliptical shape recalls that of the stone walls of Zimbabwe; they are also reminiscent of the large kraals, which, until the nineteenth century, surrounded the residences of the kings of the states in this area. Several other groups of Ethiopoid warrior herdsmen created mixed societies—herders and peasants—they themselves being the dominant group and the upper caste. Important examples are the Hima who rule over the Iru in the kingdom of Ankole and the Tutsi who rule over the Hutu in the kingdom of Rwanda.

Finally, about 1500, some groups of Luo, Nilotic pastoralists from the north, penetrated the area of the White Nile. They did not invade the whole of the area between the lakes, but their invasion had important cultural and political consequences. They seized the government of Kitara, which became Bunyoro, and, attempting to extend their conquests to the south, provoked movements as far south as Rwanda.

Communicating

The great kingdoms contemporary with the European Middle Ages were also paths for cultural communication within Africa, which was of prime importance in building up the unity of the sub Saharan civilizations. In the savannas south of the equatorial forest, the Bantu-speaking peoples whose migrations into this region have been mentioned organized political units that were sometimes called empires, because the chiefdoms that recognized the supremacy of the chief of one of them by paying tribute to him covered vast territories. Thus in the fifteenth and sixteenth centuries, the Luba hegemony extended over a large part of present-day Katanga, while the kingdom of Kongo ruled, from its capital Mbanza Kongo, the region between the Atlantic Ocean and the Rivers Zaïre, Bengo and Kwango.

Even more numerous were the exchanges facilitated by the city-states that arose, flourished and fought and succeeded each other in the Sudan region between the Sahara and the forest, the Atlantic and the Nile. The kingdom of Ghana, mentioned in a ninth-century Arabic text, was rich in gold and the work of its artisans and influenced a wide area from its capital on the site of Kumbi. This town, built entirely of stone, had a large and prosperous population and was comparable to European cities of the same time; it was conquered in 1240 by Sundiata, the Malinke ruler of Mali, the kingdom that was to succeed Ghana as the dominant power of the Western Sudan. Mali at its height in the fourteenth century stretched from the Atlantic Ocean to Gao. In addition to its capital, Mali, it included the cities of Timbuctu and Djenne. In the next century Songhai became the dominant power in the Sudan.

Thus there was much contact and borrowing in the interior of Africa. Even the greatest obstacle, the dense equatorial forest that extends over eight degrees of latitude from north to south, was no barrier. And where the nature of the soil and its vegetation made movement easy, there was much traveling: bands of warriors like the Msiri's Sumbwa, migrating peoples like the Bantu cultivators and the Luo pastoralists, conquering states like the Lunda and the Songhai and traders like the city-dwellers of the Sudan. All these were carriers of Africanity, for they transmitted social traditions from region to region, from one civilization to another. And when one society adopted one of these cultural fragments from another, a resemblance between the two societies resulted. Multiple contacts produce many resemblances, the totality of which in the end constitute an important common quality. This, together with a similarity of techniques, is the second basis of Africanity.

Being Hard to Reach

If this process of intense cultural exchanges accentuated the unique quality of Africa, it is because it occurred in a closed system. To the same degree that contacts within Africa were frequent, contacts with the world outside Africa were infrequent.

Black Africa is a country of difficult access: to the north the desert, extending right across the continent, and on all other sides a coastline with few indentations, offering few havens for ships. Its rivers are not easy routes to the interior; a bar at the mouth often makes them hard to enter, the delta is full of small islands with shallow water between them or waterfalls prevent boats from going very far upstream. The shore is either barren desert or covered with thick forest. After landing, new obstacles appear. The terrain is rarely passable for wheeled vehicles; the many areas infested with tsetse fly, which carry animal trypanosomiasis, prevent the use of horses or other beasts of burden. Until the beginning of this century it was almost impossible to travel in the interior of Africa other than on foot. Finally, the climate, almost everywhere extreme—very wet or very dry— was harsh, and the country was often unhealthy.

These obstacles do not completely account for the isolation of the African interior, for they are not unsurmountable. In other parts of the world similar difficulties were overcome. Even in Africa they did not prevent European penetration in the nineteenth century. And this was not because the explorers of that period had an easier task. Except for quinine, discovered in 1829, which provided an effective preventive measure against malaria, the means at their disposal were essentially the same as those that could have been used in the seventeenth or even the sixteenth century. Why, then, this isolation?

Exporting Valuables and Men

The reason is that the valuables that Africa could offer the world before the nineteenth century were already reaching their foreign markets. There was no point in undertaking dangerous and costly expeditions into the interior when goods could be obtained at the boundaries of Black Africa, the two ocean coasts and the edges of the desert.

What the world expected from Africa, from ancient times to the sixteenth century, was luxury goods: rare products and curiosities, both destined for the wealthy minority of Arab and European societies, especially those within the Mediterranean ambit. These goods were precious substances, such as gold— before the discovery of America, the Sudan region was the main supplier of gold to the Mediterranean world—ivory and ebony, spices such as pepper and resins such as incense and gum. The curiosities that enhanced the prestige of aristocratic homes were live animals captured in the forest and savannas or, lacking these, skins of wild animals, ostrich plumes and "unicorn" horns. There were also dwarfs and giants or just handsome young men whose gracefulness and black skins would look impressive in livery in their masters' colors.

From the sixteenth to the nineteenth century, Africa's most important export was labor, that is, slaves. From the Portuguese-owned African islands, sugar cane was taken to Brazil; and the work force followed. Then came the plantations of the West Indies, and next those of the Southern United States. The number of slaves who left West Africa for the New World in these four centuries is estimated at from eighteen to twenty-four million.*

What interests us at the moment is that contact with the outside world, and the export of luxury goods and "labor," did not bring the interior of Africa out of its cultural isolation, because these contacts were limited to the periphery of the continent and because the things given in exchange for goods and men were of little real use to Africa.

Foreign merchants came to seek these goods at certain points on the boundaries of Black Africa—ports and caravan stations— to which the goods were brought from forests and savannas, villages and camps. The earliest text concerning the east coast trade is a guide for navigators, the *Periplus of the Erythrean Sea*. It probably dates from about A.D. 110 and mentions a certain number of *emporia* on the coast of what is now Somalia. This term *emporion* used by the Greek sailor is exactly right to designate all the establishments where, up to the nineteenth century, Africans and foreigners met: places of exchange and depots where merchandise was collected to await the next ship or caravan. Thus contacts were very limited: they were temporary, commercial and between small groups of foreigners and Africans. Also, the authorities in the societies who lived near these emporia were careful to retain their privileged position as intermediaries and formed a screen between the outside world and the continent. Even the slaves were not captured by European slave traders. They were bought from the chiefs of the coastal tribes, who themselves organized expeditions into the interior.

These almost stealthy relations between Africa and the outside world in the peripheral emporia were longest lasting and most fruitful in two regions: the cities of the sub-Saharan steppe and Kongo. In the former, Maghreb merchants settled permanently, and exchanges were not limited to trade but extended to religion, science and literature: Timbuctu and Djénne in the Middle Ages were cultural centers where civilizations from

* Henri Brunschwig, *L'Avènement de l'Afrique noire du XIXe siècle à nos jours*. Armand Colin, Paris, 1963, p. 16.

south and north of the Sahara met and enriched each other. However, even here the relationship was screened: luxury goods belonged by right to the sovereigns, who directly controlled their exportation.

The mouth of the Zaïre (later called the Congo) was discovered in 1482 by the Portuguese. At the same time they discovered a well-organized, rich and powerful state, the kingdom of Kongo, where they were well received. A relationship of alliance was established between the kings of Kongo and of Portugal, one that was very different from the colonial relationship to come in the nineteenth century: young Kongo aristocrats went to study in Lisbon; European craftsmen—smiths, masons, farmers, even printers—settled in Kongo; a Kongo bishop was ordained in 1521; an ambassador to the Pope was accredited. It was more or less an agreement of cooperation. But it did not last long; Portugal turned to other overseas enterprises in India, Morocco and Brazil and in 1510 started the trade in slaves for the plantations of America.

Being Isolated

Thus relations between Africa and the outside world remained superficial, and even when they were more than mere commercial relationships, as in the cities of the Sudan and the kingdom of Kongo, they did not break the isolation of the interior of Africa.

I spoke of trade relationships; sometimes the values of the goods exchanged were so unequal that the word "trade" seems to be a euphemism. Here too we must distinguish between the cities of the region between the desert and the forest—and its extension to the Benin Gulf—and the emporia of the two coasts.

From the north, the trans-Saharan caravans brought salt, cloth, dates, figs, arms and copper. The most important use of this metal was to cast in bronze the magnificent Benin heads of the fourteenth and fifteenth centuries; in the following century the famous Benin mural plaques were cast in metals imported from Europe by sea.* The Indian Ocean and Atlantic ports

* W. and B. Forman and Philip Dark, *Benin Art.* Batchworth Press, London, 1960, p. 24.

received cotton goods, glass beads, alcohol and arms (usually obsolete). These were the "trade goods": cheap, inferior consumer goods. These were the goods exchanged for slaves in the transatlantic trade. Considering the pure economics—not to mention its inhumanity—the returns on the "export of labor" to the New World were of extremely small value. Now, slaves constituted the essential labor force for the plantations that were for a long period the only source of wealth for large areas of America. The slave trade meant the exploitation not only of the workers themselves but also of those who sold them, for a one-way trade is no longer commerce but fraud.

For the last two thousand years, Black Africa gave more than it received. Its balance sheet is weighted on the credit side. This economic deficit is less important than the cultural isolation that went with it. This isolation enabled Africanity to ripen, consolidate and differentiate itself from other cultural worlds of the same order. But this originality cost dear: the relative poverty of certain sectors of the African civilizations, especially in their techniques, was caused by isolation.

For cultures are enriched much more by borrowing than by invention. According to an American anthropologist's estimates, no culture presently existing owes more than ten per cent of its elements to the inventions, past and present, of the members of the society to which it belongs. The same holds true for the great traditions, such as those of Western Europe, which pride themselves on their creativity: they have assimilated much more than they have created.* Because the Mediterranean was a crossroad where so many cultural streams met, the civilizations that developed around it were rich and complex. Wherever groups have lived withdrawn into themselves, some aspects of their way of life or their cultural equipment have remained rudimentary. This is not, as was believed for a long time, because of a mental inferiority, but because their isolation prevented them from participating in social traditions other than their own.

* Ralph Linton, *The Study of Man.* Appleton-Century, New York, 1936, pp. 325 ff.

As we have seen, African societies interacted with each other in many ways. Even though some groups, especially in the forest clearings, lived far apart and away from major population movements, intra-African contacts were varied, many and frequent. This favorable situation contrasts strongly with the great isolation of the continent as a whole. Not until the end of the nineteenth century did a movement begin which was destined, a few decades later, to open Africa to the world and the world to Africa.

Being Penetrated

This final experience is also an experience common to all Africa. It is the modern component of Africanity. Up to this point the common quality of African culture seems to have been founded on a similarity of subsistence techniques and the diffusion of many elements through multiple intracontinental contacts, while its special nature was due to its isolation. These three mechanisms operated for centuries and constituted Africanity for most of its history. However, it would be a distortion to restrict this to traditional Africa. Africanity did not become fixed in 1885; it is a dynamic reality that is still developing. Contemporary Africa has, since the end of the nineteenth century, assimilated the consequences of an experience which, though not identical, were very similar everywhere south of the Sahara: its participation in the second great cultural mutation of humanity, the birth and diffusion of industrial techniques.

For this is the profound meaning of colonization and political independence. These two phenomena are the African manifestations on the social and political level of the worldwide Industrial Revolution. Its first result was to break the isolation of the interior of Africa.

Until the industrial period, what the outside world expected to get from Africa—luxury goods and men—had been supplied on its periphery. It was not necessary to overcome the difficult though not insuperable obstacles surrounding "darkest Africa." But the industrialization of Western Europe, especially Great Britain, made penetration essential.

The development of industrial technology is a leap forward that has only two precedents in human history: the invention of tools, which marks the simultaneous emergence of humanity and culture, and the development of agriculture and domestication of animals. Through the domestication of plants and animals the productivity of natural resources and human energy was multiplied; the quantity of goods produced was so greatly increased that the same territory could feed a much larger population, some members of the population specialized in activities that were not directly productive, large settlements grew up and new political forms arose. Compared to hand craftsmanship, industry represents just as great a leap in the quantity of goods produced. By the use of new sources of energy—steam engines, internal combustion motors, electric generators, nuclear reactors—of mechanically complex equipment and of sophisticated organization, the volume of goods that can be produced is out of all proportion to what craftsmen can make.

The effects of industry have already spread far beyond the domain of techniques. On this new foundation a new civilization is being built before our eyes, but not without difficulties. Before discussing the place of Africa in this civilization of the present and the future, let us return to the nineteenth century, when Africa felt the first repercussions of European industrialization.

Being Drawn in

Consumer goods were the first to be mass-produced. The economic system was that of capitalism in the phase of free enterprise and fierce competition. To survive, each enterprise could not allow itself to be outdone by its competitors. Consequently it was essential to produce large quantities and pay low salaries in order to sell large quantities of goods at a low price. These various economic imperatives produced an interest in Africa that had not previously existed. Africa was a rich source of raw materials for primary manufacturing industries: cotton for cheap textiles; palm oil for soap, candles and lubricating oils; rubber, the development of which was so greatly stimulated by the automobile; cocoa, coffee and other "colonial goods," the cultivation of which was especially favored by the climatic conditions of tropical areas. Thus Africa could supply cheap raw materials (it was well known from the performance of slaves on American plantations that a good source of labor existed). It could also supply foods cheap enough for the European working classes to buy, and so raise their standard of living without wage increases. Finally, in Africa there were consumers of European products for which new markets had constantly to be found (since the wages the African workers received were in fact devoted to the purchase of goods imported from Europe).

What competitive capitalist industry now required from Africa could not be supplied by mere peripheral contacts. Plantations had to be equipped, a labor force had to be recruited, eventually by conscription, roads to the ports and from the ports to the consumers had to be laid out and a monetary economy had to be established so that European consumer goods could be sold. All this required strong control over the whole continent. Colonial-type imperialism, that is, the extension of the political sovereignty of a European country over African territories, became the juridical form of this control. Although some such annexations had occurred prior to 1885, this date may be taken to mark the beginning of political colonization. In this year the Conference of Berlin met. Here the European powers interested in Africa set up the rules of their political game (for example, the rule that possession of the coast gives a right to possession of its hinterland or that actual occupation of a territory is necessary for the rights of one country to be recognized by the others).

Given a free hand with regard to its European partners, each of the powers set itself the task of effectively occupying the territories it coveted. The obstacles previously regarded as insurmountable were quickly overcome. Recognizing the authority of African kings and chiefs, European military expeditions hastened to conclude with them "treaties of friendship and protection" in the name of their governments. These agreements, the full scope of which was not realized by the African rulers—how could it have been otherwise?—were very quickly regarded as conferring full sovereign rights on the European "protectors." Curiously enough, and very indicative of the primacy of the economic viewpoint in the minds of the European governments, they usually began the colonization process by conceding the exercise of a fairly large part of their sovereign rights to private companies, which were to be responsible for the administration of vast territories in return for exploitation privileges. Thus colonial expansion progressed without any cost to the taxpayer in Europe. For various reasons the rule of the concession-holding companies was not very successful, and the administration of the colony was taken over gradually by a body of officials representing the European government involved.

This necessity for political domination became even clearer when the material equipment was also produced by European industry. The heavy steel industry manufactured rails, equipment and machines. Again, raw materials were required, and the mineral wealth of Africa was discovered. Markets, too, were required: African mines were fitted out, railroads and river and seaports were constructed. Mining enterprises and large-scale public and private works made necessary, or at least highly desirable, the political occupation of the African interior, that is, colonial imperialism.

It was thus that Africa emerged from its isolation. Industrial technology conferred on Africa a value it had not previously possessed. The Europeans, spurred by self-interest, penetrated savannas and forests and took possession of Africa and its wealth, which had so long remained undiscovered.

Being Ruled

Not all the West invaded Africa in this way; it was only certain groups from some European countries: civil servants, agents of commercial or industrial enterprises, settlers, missionaries. These four groups presented a picture of Europe that was at the same time significant and distorted. The public image of the civil servants in colonial Africa was made visible in a very different way from that of officials in Europe. Although they were civilians they wore uniforms (even in specialized branches such as the medical or veterinary services); their effective powers were more extensive; their fields of competence were almost universal: Within his designated territory, the district commissioner or administrator was responsible for public order, collecting taxes, maintaining roads, organizing agriculture, in fact, for almost the whole of social life. This considerable power came to him from above: he was accountable for it only to his superiors, and he exercised it in authoritarian fashion over the people he administered. This political relationship had ceased to exist in its totality in Western Europe at the end of the nineteenth century and the beginning of the twentieth.

Being Exploited

At this time the large private enterprises in Europe paid very little attention to the standard of living of their workers, and the workers' claims had no chance of success unless they were supported by strikes. In Africa, commercial and mining companies cared even less about their employees, and a strike was considered a crime directed at public order. On the other hand, the traditional subsistence economy that persisted everywhere greatly reduced the employers' domination of their workers: Africans could return to their villages and live as before by cultivating the land. Hence the necessity for conscription and forced labor. Moreover, the social and cultural gap between the supervisory, technical and administrative personnel and the workers was much wider than in Europe: language, life-style, access to consumer goods, skin color, all set up much more obvious barriers between worker and management.

The farmer settlers sought in Africa the free, generous style of life the great landowners had enjoyed in Europe, which was becoming increasingly more difficult to maintain there. They had a sense of adventure and risk, the desire to succeed in a difficult undertaking. Only a few areas were suitable for the establishment of large farms—Southern Africa, the Kenya highlands, the Great Lakes region—and even there the soil was not very rich, and the export routes often were long and transportation costly. The price of the goods produced could compete in world markets in most cases only because of cheap, plentiful African labor. Not all those who put down roots in Africa with the intention of staying there permanently—the settlers—were farmers. Some set up medium-sized manufacturing, industrial or commercial enterprises. If they were not quickly successful, they stagnated for a while, then disappeared; there was no middle way between success and failure.

Being Proselytized

While in Europe Christianity was losing its influence over the working masses, an intense missionary movement was developing in Africa. It was a religious commando attack, aiming at extirpating "superstitious and idolatrous" practices and converting whole groups. What Christianity entailed was quite different in nineteenth-century Africa and in Europe of the same period. In Europe, the social structures were regarded as compatible with Christianity, and the clergy tried to make Christians conform to their beliefs through personal conviction; in Africa, the missionaries believed that their task was to create Christian societies, while waiting for the traditional social institutions (polygamy, "fetish" cults, "immodest" clothing, "erotic" dances) to disappear. Converts had to be formed into new groups in villages near missionary posts. Moreover, these Christian establishments aroused in the Catholics nostalgic memories of the "centuries of faith" when the Church dominated civil society. Thus Christian activity in Africa went beyond the religious sphere. Missions aimed at establishing a new way of life; to promote it they organized elementary education, they made their posts into agricultural enterprises, they exercised political influence over colonial administrations.

Through these four channels—officials, commercial and industrial agents, settlers and missionaries—a powerful, conquering, aggressive Europe imposed itself on Africa. This Europe in Africa was perhaps an authentic but certainly a simplified image of Europe in Europe; hardly anything was the same except its active, dominating characteristics: the will to power, the pursuit of wealth, the cult of efficiency. To achieve its expansion it had decided to overcome any obstacle.

Policies and practices differed according to the European country—Great Britain, France, Germany, Belgium, Italy, Portugal—and the African territories concerned and changed several times during the three-quarters of a century of colonization. But these differences were only variations on the same theme. Africanity was reinforced by this common experience of all Africa: colonization.

Resisting

This experience did not long remain passive. After suffering the impact of the superior strength of the industrial West and being overcome for a time by the mastery of nature displayed by the Europeans, Africa pulled itself together: its peasants, subject to the poll tax and to forced labor on the construction of railroads and roads, recruited "voluntarily" to work in plantations and mines far from their villages, realized they were being exploited. The chiefs, who had become subordinate officials in the colonial administrative hierarchy, became aware that their power was illusory. The wise men, humiliated by the triumph of Christianity, which abolished and despised their customs and their world view, felt strongly the loss of their dignity. The colonial Whites, full of a naïve feeling of superiority, thought this resentment unfair: did they not deserve gratitude since they were bringing the only real civilization to a land where only savagery and barbarism had reigned?

So that Africans could pay taxes and become consumers of European products, a monetary system was introduced. It brought the possibility of unlimited increase in wealth, which was, if not impossible, very difficult to achieve in an agricultural economy. After consuming what he needed, the producer could rarely make use of the surplus except to acquire dependents; this would give him rank in the sphere of politics. Money, on the other hand, can be used in any way, and especially to improve the standard of living. The goods produced in huge quantities by industrial techniques are there—many, varied and desirable. The well-paid Europeans in the colonies enjoyed them obviously and smugly. The wages of the best-paid Africans allowed them only a minimal share of consumer goods and investments. To give some idea of the difference in pay, let us give a few figures from the last decade of colonization: in 1952 in Southern Rhodesia, the average earnings of the Africans (92 per cent of the population) were 7 per cent of the average earnings of the Europeans (8 per cent of the population); in 1955-56, in Kenya, the Africans (almost 99 per cent of the population) received 5.37 per cent of industrial and commercial earnings; in 1954, in the Belgian Congo the Africans (about 99.5 per cent of the total population) earned 2.5 per cent.* Such inequalities were hard for the Africans to bear; even though they did not know the Marxian theory of values they were well aware that labor contributed to the prosperity of enterprises to a degree far out of proportion to the benefits it obtained from them.

The Africans' resentment found support in world trends that finally began to reach Africa. The aim of colonial expansion in the nineteenth century was to make of Africa an economic dependency of Europe. The contact necessitated by this movement had an effect that the colonists did not foresee, and they soon were unable to control it. The functioning of administration and enterprises required the training of a subordinate African personnel able to speak, read and write a European language. The thirst for education spread fast, for in the colonial situation the saying "knowledge is power" is clearly shown to be true. To attract young people the missionaries organized primary schools. Moreover, this pressure for education met certain demands of evangelization: to learn the catechism, it was important to be able to read; to give up pagan practices, it was useful to be able to set against them the superiority of the literate person. Despite the screens of administrative and religious paternalism, the ideas of national independence, individual liberty and human equality spread and made colonial domination still less acceptable.

Participating in the World's Life

Thus the whole of Africa reacted to colonization basically in the same way and almost at the same time. It became aware of

* Bureau international du travail, ed., Les Problèmes du travail en Afrique. B.I.T., Geneva, 1958, pp. 317-21.

itself and of its unity, and it exerted on several colonial powers, especially after 1945, stronger and stronger pressures to obtain the political independence of various colonial territories. Between 1956 and 1966 thirty-one states were formed from former colonial territories (sixteen in 1960 alone).

Even more than in the past, African history is a single history from the beginnings of colonization to independence. Through accession to national sovereignty and attainment of membership in the United Nations, the new states receive legal recognition of their entry into world society. This is the critical event of the recent cultural history of Africa. For the first time in millennia Africa emerges from its isolation. This was achieved only through the great technical mutation of the Industrial Revolution. From this time on, Africa, like the rest of the world, is integrated into the mainstream of cultural intercourse. Like the rest of the world, it can share the cultural heritage of humanity.

Certainly these cultural exchanges will deeply affect Africanity. Formed from common experiences, both ancient ones from the traditional past and modern ones from colonization, Africanity is rich and varied in content. The early years of independence seem to be an especially fitting time to briefly take stock of this content.

City dwellers in Kinshasa, Zaïre

Two cattle herders in the mountains of Itombwe. Kivu province,
Zaïre

Two Tutsi noblemen meeting. A Hutu servant brings his master's gifts, a pot of banana beer. Shwemu, Rwanda

The chief of the Sumbwa tribe, Tanzania

Urban dweller in Kinshasa, Zaïre

A potter. Nyanza, Rwanda

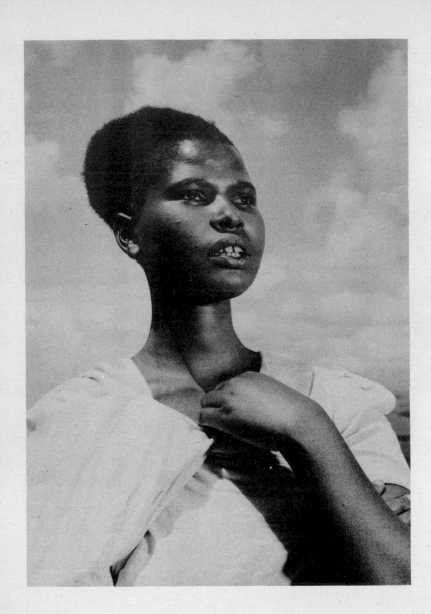

Nyirampfamasika, a Tutsi singer. Butare, Rwanda

City dweller in Kinshasa, Zaïre

Ryangombe ritual. This man personifies a mythical hero of Rwanda, Ryangombe. Shwemu, Rwanda

Sumbwa hunters, Tanzania

Antoine Munongo, the chief of the Yeke tribe. Bunkeya, Katanga
province, Zaïre

Chief, Congo-Brazzaville

THE CONTENTS OF AFRICANITY

Africanity is not a mysterious "essence," not an esoteric body of knowledge, not a configuration of characteristics; it is the totality of cultural features common to the hundreds of societies of sub-Saharan Africa. We have tried to show that this common whole is based on a similarity of existential experiences—from the cultivator's patient struggle to make a living from a rather unfavorable environment to reactions to colonial domination—and on the many cultural exchanges that took place in the interior of the continent.

The content of Africanity is the result of this double process of adaptation and diffusion. It is made up of elements belonging to various dimensions of culture: economic organization, family structure, political institutions, philosophical concepts, religions and rituals, graphic and plastic arts, the arts of movement, sound and speech. It is not easy to list these elements; every generalization calls up exceptions, requires modification, suggests reservations. For the last forty years cultural anthropologists have been trying, through their field work, to obtain a close, detailed knowledge of individual societies and how they function. Thus we become, like the actual members of one of these societies, more sensitive to its uniqueness than to its similarities to other societies, and we fear that statements about the whole continent will falsify reality. Of course, no such statement takes entirely into account such and such reality observed from close by, but we must recall that on the other hand we may be unable to see the forest for the trees. A small-scale map that shows the relief of a whole continent on one page is not false; it enables us to grasp just as genuine a reality as that depicted by much more detailed relief maps. It gives an overall view the latter cannot provide. As long as we know that the thick continuous line that marks the Andes from the top to the bottom of the map of South America is only a sign showing the general direction of the complex relief patterns of various altitudes, directions and profiles, we need not hesitate to draw it.

Becoming an African

The African child is born Black but becomes African. The human and physical environment that gradually reveals itself to him and that gradually broadens around him is different from the existential environment of the American or European child. This begins very soon after birth. For the first months of his life —and often for more than a year—the African baby is in constant physical contact with his mother. She carries him, often skin to skin, on her hip or her back; she gives him the breast whenever he is hungry. Developmental psychology has shown the prime importance of first experience in the development of personality. This constant contact with the mother, the source of warmth, food and comfort, gives the young African a much greater sense of security than the Western child enjoys, alone in his crib, fed on schedule and, if he is bottle-fed, in amounts determined by impersonal formulas. It would be rash to draw from this single feature conclusions regarding the modal personality of African and Western adults, for this depends on many other factors, but it is certain that from their first contact with the world the children of Africa all receive one response that is very different from that received by children of Europe and North America.

When the child is weaned—very late by Western standards—

and he can get around independently, his human horizon broadens more rapidly than that of the European or American child. The latter is still confined within his nuclear family: father, mother, brothers and sisters. Relationships with relatives by blood and marriage are not very close, and, besides, relatives usually live some distance away. The African child has only to take a few steps in his village to visit several people who can substitute for his father, mother, brothers and sisters, and they will treat him accordingly. Thus the child has many homes in his village, and he is simultaneously giver and receiver of widespread attention.

Finding One's Place among Kin

As he grows older, he perceives the importance of all these relatives, and he learns the subtleties of different behavior appropriate to each of them. He is thus introduced into the kinship system of his society. Whatever its norms, this system is the primary network of relationships in which each individual finds his place. While in many non-African societies one defines a person by his nationality, his profession, his social class or his religion, in Africa one first states whose descendant he is.

Filiation is determined sociologically and biologically. Biological ascent as one goes back from one generation to the preceding one, doubles the number of one's lineal relatives: two parents, four grandparents, eight great-grandparents and so on. Thus in even a fairly large group one would soon arrive at the point where all individuals had the same ancestors; this would make it impossible to establish any distinction between individuals on the basis of ancestry. Therefore each society chooses from among the biological ancestors which ones will be taken into account and which ones will be neglected. The choice is made between two basic systems: patrilineal and matrilineal. In the first case the filiation of an individual is determined only by the male line: his father, his father's father, etc.; in the latter only in the female line.

Through his father or his mother the child is, of course, connected to several ancestors in the same line. In this continuous chain, certain ancestors distinguished by prestigious deeds were chosen by their descendants as forefathers to be referred to with pride. Each of these ancestors may be regarded as the apex of a triangle with a base that broadens with each generation; the triangle constitutes the total of his descendants, that is, a lineage all of whose members feel a close solidarity. The living are united with the dead because the strength of the ancestors is transmitted through them; they are united amongst themselves because they share the same life.

Depending on Lineage

This union is expressed by the individual's strong dependence on the lineage. The lineage is organized. Its head is the man who, because of his generation, is the closest to the ancestor; but he does not reign as a despot. All important questions are discussed by the heads of the families of the lineage. Long discussions aim at reaching unanimous agreement, which is preferred, even at the cost of a compromise, to a decision imposed, even by a majority. This explains, in part at least, the special form of political democracy introduced into Africa in the constitutions of the independent states. Anglo-Saxon style parliamentary democracy, in which the party that has received the majority of the votes is in power, while the minority party constitutes the opposition, did not take root in Africa. There may be various reasons why the new nations refused to pour their political life into the molds imposed, or at least bequeathed, by the former colonial powers. But it is certain that the majority rule of the Western democratic type is not in harmony with the unanimity rule of African democracy. The latter is deeply rooted in procedures that have been institutionalized for centuries in lineage councils.

Although the child is never crushed by the corporate authority of his lineage, he is subjected to a strong, all-pervading pressure. The umbilical cord is never completely severed, simply because the lineage provides—and most often it is the only provider—for the essential needs of each of its members. When they reach marriageable age, physiologically and socially, boys and girls find a mate through the lineage. The new family is given the use of a field that it cultivates to feed itself. If misfortune strikes—a bad harvest, an epidemic among stock—kinship solidarity comes into play. If the head of the family dies prematurely, his dependents are taken care of by other members of the lineage.

Playing One's Roles

The young child gradually becomes aware of all this as he grows up. He also learns to distinguish within the lineage the various relatives toward whom he must behave in different ways. In early childhood the closest person is his mother. Whether she is the link that ties the child to his ancestor (in a matrilineal system) or whether she is the father's wife bringing her fertility to his lineage (in a patrilineal system), to the child the mother is the relative to whom he owes affection and respect, the person to whom he first entrusts himself. This is especially true for girls, who, until their marriage, live under the direct influence of their mother. From the mother one expects not authoritarian behavior but protection.

In a patrilineal system the behavior expected by a father of his children is obedience. As long as the father is alive, his sons, even when they are grown up and married, remain minors. Until their father dies they treat him reverently and submissively, that is, without taking full responsibility for themselves. For as long as one has to obey, it is the person who commands who incurs ultimate responsibility. The paternalism that arose from the colonial situation found support in this traditional paternalism, which kept some men permanently dependent on their fathers. In a matrilineal system, it is not, as might be expected, the mother who exercises authority over her children. The mother's brother represents the ancestral figures of the lineage: his sister's children must obey him; they also will inherit from him. The maternal uncle receives the bride wealth when his nieces marry, and he supplies it when his nephews take wives. However, the father's role is not reduced merely to that of begetter. He lives with his wife and children, and at least while the children are small, he necessarily exercises some authority over them at home. Later, too, he will be consulted about problems concerning his children. However, final authority belongs to his brother-in-law. This division of power between the father and the uncle is bound to cause tensions in the child's social environment. Matrilineality and patrilineality are not equally represented in African societies. The latter descent principle is much more widely seen than the former.

The behavior of the African child toward his grandparents is expected to express intimacy slightly tempered by the respect owed to all old people. Between alternate generations there is some degree of complicity, expressed by joking, great familiarity and much indulgence. The grandfather looks beyond his son—to whom he is of necessity opposed at times—to his grandson, who he does not have to discipline and who is the proof of the perpetuation of his lineage and thus of his survival in the lineage.

Among the boys and girls of his own generation, to whom he is connected by kinship or marriage, the young African quickly learns to distinguish between those toward whom he has to behave with a certain reserve and those he is allowed to treat with familiarity. These categories are set up mainly in relation to the prohibition and the possibility of marital unions. The incest prohibition is the basic rule. It applies not only to descendants of the same couple, but also to all descendants of the lineage ancestor. This means that in a patrilineal system the boy must treat with reserve his sisters, his half-sisters (the daughters of his father by wives other than his mother) and his patrilateral parallel cousins (his father's brothers' daughters), while he can play much more freely with his cross-cousins, both matrilateral (his mother's brothers' daughters) and patrilateral (his father's sisters' daughters) and his matrilateral parallel cousins (his mother's sisters' daughters).

Between other kinship categories, behavior the meaning of which is less clear is also socially determined. Thus among the Amba, on the border of Zaïre and Uganda, joking relationships exist between a man and his mother's brother and, reciprocally, between a man and his sister's son. The maternal uncle may laugh at the young man and address him with coarse remarks and even insults. The nephew cannot respond in like manner, but in return he may help himself to anything belonging to his uncle. He must not ask for it, he may simply seize it. Thus in laughing at one's nephew one risks losing one's property, and by seizing one's uncle's things one brings upon oneself vigorous verbal retaliation.*

Being Rooted in Kinship

Thus an African child's first experience of the world of human relations reveals to him a highly structured and highly protective network. He is guided in his conduct, since he knows in advance what each of his relatives expects of him and what he can expect in return. He is never isolated, since several persons are assimilated into one parental role (his father's brothers are assimilated, by extension, into the role of father; his mother's sisters into the role of mother; his patrilateral uncles' daughters into the role of sister). He owes his place in this network of rights and obligations, which is also a network of solidarity, to the fact that he is one of the descendants of a famous ancestor. This creates the most fundamental ties between him and the other descendants of that ancestor.

In the societies of the civilization of the clearings—that of the isolated cultivators in the great Atlantic and equatorial forests—kinship-based groups constitute the only social organization. Villages are based on lineages. Elsewhere there are social units based, not on kinship, but on political power, territory, production or voluntary association. But no African society to my knowledge is lacking in kinship groups or regards them as unimportant. Everywhere the African is first defined by reference to his ancestor. This is why lineage and its solidarity constitute an important content of Africanity.

This is not due to chance. Hunting and gathering, agriculture on poor soils, nomadic pastoralism, all these means of produc-

---

* Edward H. Winter, *Bwamba. A Structural-Functional Analysis of a Patrilineal Society.* Heffer, Cambridge, England, (c 1956).

tion were widespread in Africa. They provided subsistence for small groups only. If a group becomes too large it has to split, since its method of exploiting its environment has low productivity and requires the use of large areas. Thus a few families are enough to form a group that works and lives together. After several generations the descendants can relate themselves to a common ancestor. Under these circumstances it is not surprising that the kinship group forms the basic framework of society, since it is usually the only possible one. In more favorable economic conditions, other groups are added, but they do not replace the kinship group.

Going Back to the Ancestor

At the time he is living within the solidarity of the lineage, the young African is introduced to the ancestor cult, which is the projection of that social reality into the sphere of collective representations.

For it is as a member of a lineage that the individual defines himself and exists as a member of society; he owes everything to his ancestors. All over Africa, rituals evoke and symbolize this abstract truth, which is also an everyday experience. In expressing his gratitude to the ancestor and asking him to watch over his descendants, the African is merely transposing a social reality to the level of ideas and attitudes. These concepts are not naïve beliefs but the interpretation of deep truths.

In the rich body of African sculpture, which reached its highest development in the Atlantic and equatorial forests, there are many ancestor figures. These statues, some of which are great works of art universally admired by artists, critics and art historians, teach us much about the way the Africans conceived of their ancestors. These statues are figurative, but they aim to depict beings not as they are seen but as they are thought of. The sculptor transmits to us "messages" that must be read. He tells us that the individuality of the ancestor does not count: he never makes a portrait. This is not because he cannot do so: if there were clumsy efforts to imitate nature, these would be apparent, but it is clear that the artist is using a different approach. Moreover, some pieces show such skill that the artist obviously could have carved a portrait if he had wished. These abstract statues evoke the basic idea of kinship: they say that to be the descendant of an ancestor is very important; to be the descendant of a certain ancestor hardly matters. Here lies a very great difference between the cult of saints and that of ancestors, cults that are often thought of as similar. Hagiography individualizes saints, and the statues that represent them are often anecdotal: Saint Martin cuts his cloak, Saint Lawrence suffers on his rack and Saint Sebastian is shot full of arrows. The ancestors are not even shown wearing the traditional dress of their society: their nakedness accentuates their universal, abstract character.

So does their pose. Seated or standing, the body is upright, perfectly vertical, the head in a line with the spine; the arms and legs are arranged symmetrically. These various features may be attributed in part to the fact that the sculptor starts out with a section of a tree trunk and carves entirely within this form, rarely adding a piece to the original block. The face has a calm, stern expression. Within these narrow limits the best sculptors still succeed in expressing intense life and restrained movement. These various sculptural features give the ancestor figures, even the small ones, a certain monumental quality that expresses stability and strength. They tell us that the lineage is the source of power.

It is also the source of life. Breasts and vulva, penis and testicles are clearly shown. The women are often pregnant or nursing. In less explicit fashion the round and angular shapes that contrast and balance each other in African statuary recall feminine and masculine characteristics. This pervading sexuality is not erotic but austere. It tells us that procreation is the life of the lineage. This stress on fertility expresses an important aspect of the life of the small groups that must rely on themselves for survival. If, as we have seen, their numbers cannot increase beyond a certain maximum, neither can they decrease to any great extent without endangering the survival of the group. The margin is narrow. A few accidents or an epidemic are enough to threaten the very existence of the group. This is why the birth of a new member of the group, girl or boy, is always celebrated.

Being in Harmony with Reality

These statues, expressing strength and fertility, tell of the primacy of these two values in the African view of the world. They also say that man as a unique individual is less important than man as a link in the chain of generations. The life of the group passes through him rather than belonging to him as his own. Pascal is not an African. Each individual in his uniqueness is not the center of the world. The god who created the universe and, in human form, shed his drop of his blood for him, does not watch over him with care and anguish. The African man sees himself more modestly as part of the great stream of life that transcends his own self.

This vital stream is even broader than the impersonal life of the lineage seen in the ancestral figures. Here we must consider another religious belief found throughout Africa, belief in a supreme god and subordinate gods, some of whom are associated with certain places or natural phenomena.

Christian missionaries, who naturally paid great attention to these beliefs, made much of the fact, with some surprise, that the supreme god was thought of as very distant and little concerned with men and their deeds. Thus he did not seem to be the ultimate controller of the moral order: men's evil deeds did not offend him directly. On the other hand, he was rarely worshipped or prayed to, while a ritual of homage and pleas developed around ancestors and subordinate gods.

This conception of the supreme god is actually less anthropomorphic than the Christian one. To understand it, let us look again at the primeval experience from which African societies developed their gods. Of course, we have no direct knowledge of this experience. But we know that Africans, like all men, were first of all hunters, and that, until the nineteenth century, most Africans lived very close to the subsistence level in small, relatively isolated communities. They obtained the material goods they needed not so much by conquering nature as by submitting to it. Untamed nature, the forest, the savanna, the bush, surrounded the hunting band's camp, the farmer's field, the lonely village. Nature, which man can never ignore, is vast and indifferent, it hurts as much as it protects, and the good man as often as the bad is in turn victim and beneficiary.

It is not unreasonable to put these two facts together—the pressure of nature on small African communities and the conception of the supreme god—and hypothesize that the latter translates the experience of the former.

Unlike Westerners, who, having succeeded in defying nature, proceed toward its complete subjugation, Africans seek harmony with nature; they achieve it by sharing in its life and strength. This is the material basis of what has been called the Bantu philosophy of vital force.

This impersonal, deified force is the ultimate reality in which all beings share. Including man. He does not assert himself against what is other than himself and his works but sees himself as part of and continuous with reality. This vision of the world, which may be reconstructed, starting from behavior, special beliefs and rituals, and which is expressed indirectly by certain myths, is manifested in ways of acting and being that are the same everywhere in Africa.

Influencing the Forces

Magic is one of these ways of acting. By means of certain words, certain gestures, certain objects, man believes he can acquire a larger share of the power that permeates the universe and can use it for his own ends. These words, gestures and objects are effective because they are charged with power. Directed by divination to socially approved goals, magic is licit and may be practiced openly. Sorcery, on the other hand, which uses the same methods, is criminal since it aims at harming others. Although magic and sorcery are derived from the African view of impersonal force, they are also a form of individual, willed action on the world. By their means, people try to influence events that are beyond rational control, such as drought and disease, but events they cannot resign themselves to suffer passively: acknowledgment that there is nothing that can be done produces unbearable anxiety. Magical thought is not peculiar to Africa. It is universal. Although we do not like to admit it, it is widespread in the West under various disguises, from fortune-telling with cards to the curing of disease by contact with relics. In Africa magical thought and the view of a world of forces go together logically.

Another attitude that fits this view of the basic unity of human life and nature concerns death. Death does not have the tragic and shocking aspect that it has in individualist traditions, where it means the annihilation of a being that is its own end—which is absurd. In Africa, death means the disappearance of a being whose ultimate reality is entirely relative to entities that existed before it and will exist after it: the lineage, the society, the world. Herein lies true reality, not in the individual. The African is never wholly separated from these entities while he is alive, and he does not see his death as a total breach with them.

Of course the African, like anyone else, knows that it is painful to leave life with its uncertain joys and sorrows, but he has always felt himself to be an integral part of the endless stream of life, and this helps him to resign himself to death. Besides, he believes in life after death. But it is hardly an attractive life. It is an attenuated ghost life; the ghosts live in a limbo for a few generations, not far from the living. The idea that life after death is temporary shows clearly an understanding that to forget the dead effaces all traces of their existence.

Thus the philosophy of participating in the total life of the world, the constant attempt to increase power, the awareness of the primacy of the group over the individual, all constitute one more aspect of Africanity. This ontological vision is expressed in many ways: in complex and esoteric bodies of knowledge, like those of the Dogon or the Fall; in agricultural rites in which the fertility of the earth and of women are worshipped together; in magical cures in which an attempt is made to heal the patient by strengthening his vital force; in the worship of gods associated with certain special places where powerful forces converge. Beneath these various expressions a common conception, rooted in the common technical and economic conditions it reflects, may be discovered.

Reaching Adulthood

By the everyday life of their family, their lineage and their village, by the precepts and occasional remarks of the elders, the African boy and girl reaching adolescence have already assimilated the essential part of their social heritage. They know their place in the network of human relations and the place of mankind in the world. In nearly all African societies, this preparation is not regarded as sufficient. Before being admitted to adult status they must undergo initiation.

This is in the first place a test that may be very painful when it includes surgical operations such as circumcision for boys and excision for girls. There may also be scarification or mutilation of the teeth, and these may constitute tribal markings. These tests must be borne without complaint. To enjoy the rights of adulthood one must be worthy of them and show that one will be able to endure the physical and mental wounds inflicted by life, the pains of childbirth and the risks of war.

It is also an education. One speaks of initiation "schools" because preparation for the ceremonies may take a long time, continuing for weeks or even months. During this period the children live apart from their usual family environment. Girls are entrusted to old, experienced women, and boys to wise, respected men. These instructors transmit and explain the maxims that later will help in solving problems concerning the behavior and manners expected by the group. African societies distrust improvisation. They seek to train individuals to adapt to their various social roles and to get along well with others rather than to develop strong personalities that inevitably produce tensions in group living. Again we acknowledge the primacy of the group over the individual. If it fits the African philosophy of man, it also expresses the social experience of small communities: when everybody knows everybody else and cannot avoid cooperating with any other member of the group, mutual adjustment is not easy and must be deliberately sought. Education by initiation is directed to this end.

Besides being a test of courage and the completion of education, initiation is also a collective ceremony. In European societies, reaching puberty is a private matter. Each girl and boy goes through adolescence to sexual maturity alone. In Africa the long initiation ceremonials dramatize this change and make it a social ritual. The community rejoices because the long apprenticeship begun at birth and served for many years has at last ended successfully. The event concerns not only the young people involved but also their lineage and their village. The promise of future generations who will ensure the perpetuation of the group and strengthen its life calls for joyful celebration.

Initiation is especially important in societies divided into age classes, an institution especially prevalent in the societies of warrior herdsmen that comprise the civilization of the spear. When a sufficient number of young men reach biological maturity, they are initiated together. Thenceforth they form a class cutting across descent groups. Its members are united for life in close solidarity. The new age class created at initiation must fulfill a certain social function, for example, that of a military war force, a function hitherto performed by the previous initiation group a few years earlier. The previous class then assumes another social function, that of government, while the one before that turns to the activities of old age. Thus the stages of life, individual in Western societies, are integrated into a social order. Age class systems do not exist in all African societies. Nevertheless, we mention them because they represent the culmination of a trend that seems to us characteristic of Africa: the division of a society into various categories of persons according to age and sex and the allotting to each of these categories a particular social task. In more familiar terms, we might say that these societies have no tendency to anarchy or even liberalism, but a strong tendency toward planning.

Getting Married

To be an adult is above all to be married, to be a mother or a father. If bachelors exist in African societies, their situation is not a normal, expected social role. Like physical infirmity or mental deficiency, cases of bachelorhood occur from time to time, but they are regarded as aberrations or misfortunes: it would be preferable if they did not exist. Thus initiation is to a large extent preparation for marriage. The duties of a wife are explained and specified to the girls; a sense of paternal responsibility is instilled in the boys. In some societies in Tanzania, the initiators teach chanted maxims the meaning of which, often obscure, is explained and even illustrated by baked clay figurines that represent or suggest the recommended or condemned behavior. It is borne in mind that along with the ideal behavior there are other behaviors it is wise to put up with. For example, the Ngu teacher tells his pupils that a husband whose wife has just given birth and who doubts the paternity of the child would do well not to increase his anxiety by useless questioning.*

Americans and Europeans are sometimes surprised or shocked by oversimplified pictures of African marriage: "People are betrothed against their will," "wives are bought." These caricatures of African matrimonial relations are based on the distortion of a reality that all the same has aspects very different from Western marriage, at least as it has been idealized since the nineteenth century.

It is true that African marriage concerns not only the couple involved: it is primarily an alliance between two kinship groups. The primacy of the lineage is clearly shown at all the stages of the long process of marriage. When a young man reaches the age at which it is customary in his society to take a wife, his father (in a patrilineal system) or his mother's brother (in a matrilineal system) holds an unofficial, or sometimes a formal, consultation with the closest relatives on the matrimonial possibilities available. The merits of various potential brides are compared. Consideration is given to the suitability or usefulness of alliance with the kinship groups of girls of marriageable age, but individual qualities are also studied. Criteria vary according to the way of life and social class: nomadic pastoralists and farmers do not share the same ideas on what constitutes an ideal bride, nor do nobles and peasants. However, all societies agree in placing the highest value on qualities that seem to guarantee

* H. Cory, *African Figurines*. Faber, London, 1956.

fertility. Thus in Rwanda virginity was regarded as an indispensable condition for future fertility and consequently was required of a bride.*

When the lineage has settled on a choice, one of its members, usually the boy's father, discreetly inquires into the feelings of the girl's lineage. This is a delicate sounding out: a refusal would involve the risk of a quarrel between the two families; a definite request can be made only when it is certain to be accepted. Somehow, therefore, the girl's family must first be allowed to make its position known in an indirect way, which cannot cause embarrassment if it should unfortunately be negative. The decision to accept or reject the suggested alliance is also taken in council by the girl's relatives. It is discreetly communicated to the boy's lineage, which, as the case may be, discontinues the process or, on the other hand, expresses its request openly in the customary form.

This procedure, common throughout sub-Saharan Africa, seems to leave out entirely the opinions of the two people involved; and indeed it is rare for their preferences to be formally expressed. But, actually, girls and boys who are sufficiently determined could cause the failure of marriage plans displeasing to one or the other of them or even impose their preferences on their lineage. Through certain relatives he especially trusted —perhaps his father's sister—the boy might indicate the girl he would like to marry and with whom he had come to a secret agreement; if his lineage opposed this union, it would be possible for him, according to the custom of many societies, to present them with a fait accompli by eloping with the girl. Then the lineage could only ratify the existing situation. By indirect means, using the influence of various relatives, a girl could effectively object to a choice she disliked.

It is certain, however, that in most cases individual preferences played a much smaller part in African marriage than in modern Western marriage: young people took it for granted that the lineage should decide whom they should marry. A new

* Jacques Maquet, *The Premise of Inequality in Rwanda*. Oxford University Press, London, 1961, p. 67.

generation of descendants of the ancestor was to be born: the new link to be formed concerned the whole lineage.

Moreover, in equalitarian agricultural societies or in the agricultural class of stratified societies—that is, in a large majority of African populations—the lineage's choice was no different from the one the individuals would have made for themselves. As in Europe, matrimonial alliances are instruments of power politics only in the political or economic aristocracy. Before the nineteenth century, political marriages occurred only in the nobility and economic ones in the rich bourgeoisie, not among the peasants.

Exchanging Women

When the lineages have reached agreement on the bride and bridegroom, they still have to negotiate the amount of goods and services that the young man is to give his father-in-law. In one form or another such payments are made in all African societies. This is the origin of the legend concerning the purchase of women, to which the Africans reply by asking whether the custom of giving a dowry in Europe means that the father is buying a husband for his daughter.

To understand the meaning of bride wealth, let us look at an ancient custom that has persisted in a few societies, the custom of exchanging women.

For the lineage, the descent group has a social reality stronger than that of the individual: the most important concern is its continuity. Now it cannot perpetuate itself alone: descendants of the same ancestor, even a remote one, are brothers and sisters and cannot marry each other. This being so, the group practices exogamy: it must seek marriage partners outside itself. In the patrilineal system, which is the more common one, brides of the lineage men must come from outside the system, and the lineage girls must leave the system to marry. Thus the perpetuation of the lineages can be ensured only by the circulation of women.

In the demographic conditions of small societies living close to the subsistence level, every girl whose fertility will ensure the

survival of a lineage other than her own is important. Regulation of the circulation of women becomes necessary. The sim-
plest form of this is exchange. When a man marries a woman,
he must give his sister to his bride's brother. Thus neither of
the lineages loses the fertility value of a woman. As it is often
difficult to fulfill the conditions of such an exchange, the brother
of the first bride may be replaced by any other man of his
lineage. The same goes for the sister of the first bridegroom.
Even so, these double marriages are not always easy to arrange.
Besides, there is another serious inconvenience: if one of the
couples does not get along and ends the marriage, the parallel
couple may also have to break up.

Compensating for the Gift of Fertility

Marriage by matrimonial compensation avoids these incon-
veniences by ensuring that the bride-giving group will be able
to obtain a bride from any lineage when one of its men needs
one. This is the essential meaning of bride wealth: the bride-
receiving lineage, instead of giving another woman in exchange,
offers goods that enable the bride-giving lineage to obtain a
woman in its turn. In some societies the bride wealth received
remains separate from inheritable wealth: it can be used only in
another marriage, to obtain a bride. This clearly shows the true
meaning of matrimonial goods.

Sometimes these goods have important economic value; sometimes their value is symbolic. In agricultural societies, they are
hoes, goats or sheep; in pastoral societies, cows; in societies
where trade and crafts are developed, skeins of spun cotton or
pieces of iron, copper or brass. In some cases the system has
become corrupt and is a means of hoarding women or getting
rich. Where there are considerable inequalities in wealth, rich
men, who are often middle-aged or old, can marry several young
women, while young men have difficulty obtaining one wife.
When a young woman lives in a town, far from her home village, one of her more or less distant relatives, who in principle
represents her lineage, may try to obtain from her fiancé a very
high bride wealth in money. Nevertheless, these abuses and cor-

ruptions of the system, should not obscure its essential significance.

In modern Western marriage, the ceremony that marks the change of status is the solemn declaration, before a public authority, of the decision of a man and a woman to choose one another as spouses. African marriage also involves a ritual, but it is not completed until the whole of the bride wealth (which may be paid off in several installments) has been remitted. This is because bride wealth transfers the rights to the woman's offspring. When a woman gives birth to a child before the compensation has been paid to her lineage, the child is regarded as a member of her lineage, not its father's.

Stabilizing Matrimonial Alliances

As an alliance between two families, a marriage must be stable so that good relationships between the lineages will not be endangered. So when a couple quarrel and want to separate, the two lineages usually put pressure on them to make up their differences. But African wisdom and realism have avoided making marriage indissoluble; Africans know that social harmony is better served in the end by the breaking of certain ties rather than by maintaining a situation that has become intolerable. The wife returns to her family either of her own accord or because her husband, wanting to get rid of her, makes her life impossible. The actual separation becomes divorce when the two lineages, after unsuccessful attempts to persuade the couple to resume their life together, resign themselves to ending the alliance by agreeing on an eventual refunding of the bride wealth. If the wife had not borne a child during the marriage, her lineage must in principle return the compensation.

Many marriages are stable, ending only with the death of one of the spouses. It has been said that in Africa there are no widows or orphans. It is certainly true that personal insecurity and loneliness are reduced to a minimum. When the father of a family dies, his wife or wives still live within the network of the dead man's lineage; they may become wives of his brothers or cousins or merely become attached to these men's families. The dead man's children, already subject to the authority of his lineage, will be supported by their uncles and continue to enjoy the same standard of life and the same education. If by some misfortune the father's lineage is far away or even extinct, the mother's lineage will take back the daughter and her children and reintegrate them.

Traditional African societies are at the mercy of the dangers and uncertainties of the human condition: sickness and old age, drought and famine. They have fewer means of defense against them than have industrialized Western societies. But they are much better than industrial societies at organizing human relationships so as to reduce tensions and anxieties. The isolation of modern Western man seems to increase as the population of his cities grow and his communications intensify; man's insecurity seems to grow greater as his mastery of the world becomes surer. The African has learned wonderfully well to make the best of his situation by developing to the utmost the possibilities of harmony and adaptation inherent in the social nature of man.

Marrying Several Wives

Of the two possible forms of polygamy, polyandry (the union of one woman and several husbands) and polygyny (the union of one man and several wives), the former does not exist in Africa. One cannot apply the term polyandry to the rather widespread custom in Africa of not regarding as adulterous sexual relationships that may occur between a woman and her husband's brothers. These relationships, which in some cases are regarded as desirable, express the unity of the lineage and the close solidarity between brothers.

Polygyny, on the other hand, is universal in Africa, not in the sense that every man has several wives but in that all African societies regard plural marriage as permissible and even desirable. This preference is not peculiar to Africa; it is, we might say, universal: among all known societies of the world, a large majority (of the order of eighty per cent) are polygynous in the sense that plural marriage is allowed and more prestigious than is monogamous marriage. In all societies, however, monogamous marriages are more numerous: the sex ratio, even modified by the high mortality of men due to their more dangerous activities, does not permit widespread polygyny even where it is highly valued and sought after.* It is the prohibition of polygyny, not its authorization, that poses a problem. The question is, rather, what are the functions of plural marriage in African societies?

The most obvious function is the economic one. The productive unit for agricultural work is, almost everywhere in Africa, the nuclear family consisting of a couple and their children. When a man has several wives, each of them, with the help of her children, cultivates her parcel of land. Thus the polygynous husband obtains more consumer goods than the monogamous husband. Plural marriage brings prosperity, and is thus a sign of wealth.

For kings and rulers the opportunity of marrying several women has an important political function. It enables them to form many alliances with powerful kinship groups that might try to seize power from those who hold it. By marrying women from different lineages, the chief can manipulate allies and practice on a large scale policies which the princely families of Europe could carry out only within the narrow limits of monogamy.

Making the Lineage Continue

By means of polygyny, a man increases the number of his descendants while sparing his wives' health by spacing out births. The high valuation of birth in the eyes of the lineage and the village brings out the importance of this function of plural marriage for African societies. Where statistics on these phenomena exist, they confirm the positive relationship between polygyny and reproduction that common sense leads us to expect.† We think this relationship should be stressed because

---

* George Peter Murdock, *Social Structure*, Macmillan, New York, 1949.
† Vernon R. Dorjahn, "The Factor of Polygyny in African Demography." *Continuity and Change in African Cultures*, ed. William R. Bascom and Melville J. Herskovits, University of Chicago Press, Chicago, 1959, pp. 109 ff.

some Catholic missionaries have held that polygyny reduces the birth rate.

The sexual significance of polygamy—the first thing that Westerners think of—obviously exists. But the pleasant variety that this provides a man is certainly not the most important function of plural marriage. The ordinary polygamous African does not live with the erotic refinements that the word "harem" suggests to us. His wives are few, two or three, and they do not live a cloistered harem life. Each has a dwelling quite apart from those of her co-wives, where she lives with her children. In aristocratic castes, sometimes, each wife of a nobleman was set up in a domain that she ruled and exploited; this was the case in Rwanda. The husband spent one or two days and nights in the residence of each of his wives in turn.

African sexuality both in and out of marriage shows moderation and control. Our Western imaginations have projected our desires and dissatisfactions onto exotic societies. Actually, licentious mores and primitive innocence exist only in these dreams. In some societies premarital chastity is required of girls, while in others very little importance is attached to the sex games and familiarities of young people. Everywhere married couples are supposed to be faithful, but not in the absolute, Western sense of the word. Thus relationships with certain partners may not be cause for punishment and compensation, though the husband may take offense at them. Such privileged partners are the members of the husband's lineage who are his close equivalents in generation and consanguinity, and of whom one would take over the wife in the case of her husband's death; they are also the husband's guests whom he sometimes invites to enjoy conjugal hospitality. We might say, without falling into the misconception we have mentioned, that the African idea of sexuality avoids dramatizing and personalizing this activity as we have been taught to do by the romantic tradition.

The intervention of kinship in marital arrangements; the custom of bride wealth, symbolizing the transfer of fertility from one lineage to another; the polygyny to increase the number of descendants; the restrictions on sexual freedom all these are features of Africanity in the sphere of family life. But the precedence of the lineage over the individual is not absolute. The safeguards that mitigate this predominance are equally part of the African heritage. They include discreet mediation by close relatives of an engaged couple, enabling them to express their preferences and if they choose, to elope; separation and divorce; acceptance of widows and care of orphans; separate dwellings for co-wives as well as relative freedom of movement; sexual tolerance before and during marriage. Thus family organization, so essential to the life of the group and the individual since it regulates reproduction and sexuality, successfully achieves, it seems, a difficult compromise between collective requirements, which take precedence, and personal preferences, which are respected to a considerable degree.

Compromise is a key word in Africanity. It is a way of settling personal disputes and conflicts of interest by trying to find a solution acceptable to both parties in that it gives each party part of what it claims. The antithesis of settlement by compromise is settlement by reference to abstract principles. The application of such principles often results in an extreme solution: one of the parties has the right and the other has nothing. This kind of solution, so satisfying to the rigid and systematic mind, is distasteful to Africans. For they know from experience gathered from generations who have lived in small communities that reconciliation is essential for cooperation and may be better achieved by negotiating than by seeking to create an ideal system. With human nature, too, one must compromise and negotiate.

Living in a Village

Until marriage the young African may live almost entirely within the framework of his lineage. Through marriage he comes into contact with a larger social world, since his bride of necessity belongs to a different kinship group.

The smallest but also the most immediate form of the world beyond the lineage is the village community. Of course some villages are populated by members of a single lineage: all those who live there are descended from the same ancestor, and the only outsiders are their spouses. But such cases are rare, or, rather, temporary. Actually when the living descendants of a distant ancestor become too numerous to live together, the descendants of a closer ancestor gather together and go to settle elsewhere, founding a new village. This new village attracts immigrants from other groups too small to form a settlement of their own, who welcome the opportunity of joining a new territorial unit. Thus a village usually comprises several kinship groups.

This communal life makes necessary a social organization based on some principle other than that of descent. The lineage patriarch holds his authority from the ancestor he represents. Because of his position in the succession of generations, he is placed between the ancestor and the ancestor's other descendants who are younger than he. How, then, can he validate his authority over outsiders?

Africans have solved this problem by a collegial authority exercised by the chiefs of the various lineages living in the village. Each represents a closely united group and can speak in its name. The chief of the lineage that founded the village has the most influence but no authority to overrule the other chiefs. The village is managed by the democratic and paternalistic methods customary in the lineage. The council of patriarchs makes decisions only after listening to the opinions of the village chiefs. In African councils every man can express his opinion, but the weight carried by an opinion depends on the status, age and prestige of the man who expresses it. This means that in effect decisions are made according to the wishes of the elders: their opinions are supported because of their moral superiority, the ancestral force reposing in them and the respect due to their age, not because they impose their views and enforce their decisions. In any case they could not do so. There is no police force in the village.

Controlling without Coercion

Of course there are many variations on the pattern of the African village we have tried to describe. When the village forms part of a broader, highly structured system, the organization becomes more complex: we shall soon study such a case. What we are describing is the local self-governing community. This social unit is very important in Africa, first because villages, even when they form part of a state organization, still retain their democratic familial character to a high degree; second because in large areas of Africa—especially in the Atlantic and equatorial forest zone—independent villages existed right up to the end of the traditional period. Of course they were only part of broader cultural systems united by a common language, legal system and religious ideas, but they were not part of the same political structure: loose bonds of alliances or allegiances did not interfere with the community life of the village.

This community life did not require the use or threat of physical coercion. How, then, could the community ensure obedience to the decisions of the elders and the rules imposed by any form of social life? By collective pressures, which can be as effective as force. When one lives in a community where everybody knows everybody else and where everybody must cooperate with everybody else at certain activities, the disapproval of others is hard to bear. It is expressed by ridicule, refusal to speak, ostracism. When people depend heavily on each other, life soon becomes unbearable, and the most obstinate delinquent has to reconcile himself with his village or else leave it. The latter alternative cannot be chosen lightly: it usually implies abandoning one's land and trying to get oneself accepted in another village. But to be effective such sanctions must assume the unanimous agreement of the group. For unless all its members participate fully in the general attitude of disapproval, the sanction loses its strength and effectiveness. This means that an arbitrary action or a harsh decision by the elders would stand little chance of being carried out properly; a little negligence or relaxation by the villagers would suffice to make it fail. Collective support is indispensable.

The play of sanctions by social pressure in the village illuminates what we might call African-type democracy. On the discussion level, the consideration and respect commanded by the high social position of certain individuals does not admit of an entirely free exchange of opinions; that is possible only among equals. It would be unfitting if everybody did not finally come round to the views of the elders. But on the execution level a genuinely convinced unanimity is indispensable. Without causing the elders to lose face by opposing them openly, the ordinary villagers—even a minority of them—can make the whole weight of their disagreement felt by the incomplete execution of unanimously approved measures. Community control of execution limits authoritarianism more effectively than free discussion of decisions.

Other sanctions ensure obedience to the rules of village life. An illness, a bad harvest, or some other misfortune occurs. The victim, with the help of the diviner, determines the cause: he has neglected certain lineage obligations and the ancestors are displeased; he has wronged someone, who is avenging himself by magic. To stop the punishment the offense must be expiated. Thus the belief in the action of the dead on their descendants and in the power of magic can effect punishment of secret violators of the social norms. These punishments are especially effective since concealed misdeeds do not escape the agents of justice.

Observation of the rules of conduct is enforced by even more indirect measures. The nonconformist or habitual troublemaker may be suspected of witchcraft. This is a very serious accusation, for the witch—one who uses magic for antisocial purposes—is a criminal deserving of death. First rumored, then hinted at and finally made public, the accusation obliges the alleged witch to exonerate himself. Often he can attempt this only by submitting to dangerous tests such as ordeal by poison or by fire.

It has been said all Africans live in villages. This is not accurate. There are camps of hunters and pastoral nomads; more important, there are cities of traders and craftsmen in the bend of the Niger (Djenne, Timbuktu, Gao), in the region between the Niger and Lake Chad (Kano, Zaria, Katsena), from the Chad area to the Nile (Goulfeil, Abeche, Djebel Uri), in the Benin gulf area (Ibadan, Oshogbo, Ife, Edo). There are also the capitals of the kingdoms of the southern savanna; from the Lozi State in the Zambezi Valley to the kingdom of Kongo on the Atlantic coast. However, it is true that the life setting of many, indeed most, Africans is the village. Thus the attitudes, ideas and behavior arising from life experience in small communities are part of Africanity: the preference for intense and numerous interpersonal relationships, a social life that appears very free but is regulated by a strong and adaptable organization and an authority that is recognized and respected but that can act only with popular consent.

Producing a Surplus

These patriarchal democracies the balance of which delights the anthropologist no doubt result from African wisdom. But they are also children of necessity. Political power, inseparable from coercion, can only arise and develop in situations where some system of enforcement can be set up. This presupposes certain specific economic conditions.

In situations where the unit of production—the nuclear family consisting of the father, his wives and their children—consumes all it produces, either directly or by exchanging part of it for other consumer goods necessary for subsistence, every adult must devote most of his effort to producing food and other goods essential for his own survival and that of his dependents. Anybody who did not farm could survive only if fed by others, which is logically impossible, since productivity is so low that each unit produces no more than it consumes. A group of individuals constituting an instrument of coercion could not arise in such a society.

This line of reasoning is borne out by the facts. The village communities in which there is no group of men devoted to the specialized task of government are poor societies that cannot spare several of their members from productive work; societies that have government officials are those in which the production of a unit exceeds its consumption. There are many such societies in Africa.

When agriculture crosses the threshold of surplus, new possibilities open up for social organization. As a broad generalization, it might be said that this threshold lies between forest agriculture and savanna agriculture. Of course even the latter produces a very modest yield. Every year there is a difficult period: before the harvest there are several weeks of scarcity. However, a family can subsist without consuming all it produces: granaries bear witness to the existence of a reserve. These are built near, but apart from, the houses; they are huge woven baskets covered with clay and supported on a wooden structure to protect the food from the damp and the depredations of small animals. The granaries hold rice, millet, sorghum, beans, peas, haricot beans and other non-perishable foodstuffs.

These foodstuffs are also easy to transport. This enables the producer to exchange the surplus from his harvest for other goods or for services. It also enables him to pay taxes, that is, to hand over to the chief the whole or a part of the surplus without economic return. Overproduction and political power are bound up together. Whether the former is the origin, the "cause" of the latter, or whether the latter gives rise to the former is a question that does not matter here. It is enough that in fact they appear simultaneously and that logically the former is a necessary condition for the latter.

Governing a Territory

African forms of government cover a very broad range, from small chiefdoms to empires with a hegemony that extends over wide areas. All these forms have certain characteristics in common. The proportion of each characteristic varies considerably in different systems of government, but the constant presence of all means that their totality delineates the political content of Africanity.

The coercive power of rulers is exercised over a certain territory. Because of blood ties, people are subject to the lineage-wide authority of the patriarch, and, because of agreements between patriarchs, they are subject to the village-wide authority of the council. As a result of the principle of the territoriality of power, they are subject to the chief. When power is based on physical sanctions it is bounded spatially and does not need validation by kinship. The principle of territorial power is very explicit in the centralized states of the Great Lakes area: here government owns the land. It possesses not only sovereignty over the land in the sense of eminent domain, which defines the relationship between the state and its national territory, but an exclusive ownership, which characterizes the relationship between an individual and his property in Western, Roman-based law.

Of course, in the many forms of governmental systems, kinship and territoriality are not as sharply distinguished as this analysis might lead us to believe. Thus the principle of descent was sometimes extended to groups larger than the lineage: the clan and the tribe. But this was a matter of mythical descent that did not lead to the same consequences as the real kinship two individuals establish with each other by tracing their ties to a common ancestor. The clan ancestor was remote, often mythical, and the links between him and the present generation could not be traced. Thus the clan was a nominal group rather than a real one: it lacked the internal organization of the lineage, ties of solidarity between the members were weak and the rule of exogamy was not applied. These various characteristics were even vaguer in the tribe. The term "tribe" is applied to a whole society all of whose members claim to be sons and daughters of the same hero, while the term "clan" is used for segments of a society of this type. When a tribe is politically organized as a chiefdom or kingdom, the principles of territoriality and kinship co-exist: the former displays the real power of the rulers, while the latter expresses the political relationship through the familiar, reassuring symbols of ancestral descent.

Ruling Alone

The monarchical form is a second characteristic of African governments. The Aristotelian idea of monarchy, "government by one man," should not be taken literally: we know well enough that there are always several rulers; but a system may be called monarchical when one of the rulers is regarded as in supreme control of coercive sanctions. This is the chief, paramount chief or king. In Africa supreme power belongs to one man, not to an assembly or a council. According to the African theory the monarch's powers are great, even absolute. First in the sense that the three branches of power distinguished by our public law—legislative, judicial and executive—are held as a unit by the sovereign chief. If he delegates them instead of exercising them himself, he can repossess them at any time and so repeal a decision given by his delegate. The monarch is also absolute in that no institution or person can set a limit to his power: often, especially in the kingdoms near the west coast, it is explicitly recognized that he has the right to dispose of the life and property of all his subjects. He can have a man executed and confiscate his goods with no justification but his own wish. Finally, he need not account for his stewardship to anybody, common people or notables.

This absolutism is part of the expressed ideology of the strongly centralized states, the wealthy city-states of the Sudan area and the pastoral kingdoms of the eastern highlands. Actually, neither there nor elsewhere could these exorbitant powers be effectively exercised, except occasionally. The great, closely united lineages constituted social forces the monarch had to respect: their rebellions often took the form of coups d'état, which sometimes succeeded. Single individuals or families could take the chance of leaving the territory if conditions of life became unbearable. Like any political power that claims to be unlimited, African absolutism was actually tempered by threats of revolt and evasion, even in cases when certain monarchs were tempted to put it into practice. Elsewhere, indeed in most cases, absolutist ideology remained on the level of an intellectual concept that no one attempts to translate into everyday behavior.

Being Identified with the People

What is the reason for so extreme an ideology? It can certainly be found, in part, in a third characteristic of supreme power in Africa: it is sacred, and sacred in a deeper sense than the power of Western monarchies based on divine right. The sovereign, by his office—and not by individual predestination, which would make him a charismatic leader—has a special position in the world of vital forces. He shares in them more than ordinary men, for he represents his people and identifies with them: in a mystical sense he *is* his community. Thus in many kingdoms, both east and west, when the king is weak or sick the strength of the whole group is in peril: harvests are less abundant, cows produce less milk, women are less fertile. For this reason the king whose weakening vitality becomes known to all the land has to kill himself, or fall asleep, as they say in the Benin Gulf kingdoms.* The king cannot die either by suicide or by natural death; like his people he is immortal. This is why when a king "goes to his last rest" the event is concealed in many societies, while in others the funerary rites deny death: from his mummified body he will be reborn in the form of an animal, which, in turn, will manifest itself in his successor. Everywhere the interregnum is a dangerous period for the society, which will recover its stability only when another monarch is appointed.

The fearsome vital force the monarch bears is also expressed in his lifetime by the very strict protocol that indicates he is apart from other men. Sometimes a special vocabulary is used to describe his ordinary activities such as drinking, eating, sleeping; he is addressed kneeling; he may not be seen but gives audience from behind a curtain. He is subject to innumerable prohibitions of all kinds. In Rwanda, when the army was fighting far away from the king's court, the monarch could not move backward for fear that such a movement would cause the warriors to retreat. Before sowing began, he would ensure germination by having intercourse with one of his wives. In Buganda, his high position in the world of the gods authorized the king to convoke certain gods to his court, to give audience to them through mediums and even to punish them by destroying their sanctuaries.†

Beliefs about the sacredness of the monarch are not everywhere elaborated to the same degree. As might be expected,

* Montserrat Palau Marti, *Le Roi-dieu au Bénin*. Berger-Levrault, Paris, 1964.
† T. Irstam, *The King of Ganda*. Ethnographic Museum of Sweden, Lund, 1944.

they are more highly developed in large state systems than in smaller chiefdoms. However, in all cases political power in its most practical form of physical coercion and economic privilege is also considered in its aspect of a vital force, that is, one in harmony with the philosophical conception of the world. This shows how deeply rooted is this African view of the universe and to what a degree it unifies apparently separate phenomena. Just as in his action on the natural environment, in the union of the sexes, in descent from an ancestor the African sees his participation in a great lifestream that links the individual with a basic reality greater than himself, so he considers political power from a philosophical point of view. The ideal chief is not an exceptional individual who realizes to the full his personal potentialities, he is, *through his office*, an indispensable inter-mediary between the life of the world and his community. In his exalted position above other men no trace is to be found of a personality cult: he is only a channel for the vital force, and, when he is no longer in a condition to fulfill this function of intermediary effectively, he must remove himself. Even for kings the human collectivity, itself part of the order of nature, takes precedence over the individual.

Succeeding by Heredity

A monarch inherits his office. Legitimacy does not originate from the choice of the subjects, though often their desires can or even must be expressed, if only indirectly. Chiefs and kings refer first of all to their genealogy to affirm their legitimacy. The ideal genealogy is one that can be traced back in a direct line, usually the male line, to the founder of the dynasty, a superman or a son of the gods come down from heaven. In Bunyoro and Rwanda changes of dynasty are carefully disguised, and court historians are responsible for preserving intact the official version of dynastic traditions.

This system of inheritance does not usually designate a single successor—for example, the oldest son of the first wife—but a class of possible successors—for example, all the sons born to the king's wives during his reign. In the Great Lakes kingdoms, especially, this gives rise to a choice among the king's sons and to competition, often murderous, among them. Through choice and competition, various social forces come into play. During the king's lifetime, his successor is not known; he is chosen immediately after the king's death by some high officials who actually represent the interests of the principal lineages. Their decision, which they present as that of the dead king, is often contested by one or another of the other possible successors who, with sufficient support, may succeed in defeating the "official candidate" and imposing himself. Thus the rigidity of the hereditary system is modified by a plurality of possible successors; the margin of uncertainty works in favor of the candidate most skilled in obtaining the support of influential groups. Here we have another manifestation of the African sense of realistic compromise.

Being a Courtier

The monarch, whether chief or king, is surrounded by various persons without whom he could not exercise his supreme prerogatives. From the viewpoint of sociological analysis, there is always a ruling group that possesses the two characteristics defining political superiority: exclusive control of physical force and disposal of wealth produced by others. From this perspective the monarch is no longer a unique ruler. He is one ruler among others, even if he is the first in importance and the perfect symbol of their collective power.

In the centralized states, the ruling group comprises several categories. The first is the court, comprising the king's immediate assistants. Because they perform the executive functions they are often referred to collectively as the central government. We prefer the word "court," which suggests the vaguer relationships arising from the sovereign's favor and the courtiers' eagerness to please him. The court includes first, the king's devoted friends, whom he trusts; second, relatives and allies who represent the lineages close to him. Toward those who might lay claim to the throne the king is understandably most distrustful: his potential rivals live at the court to be closely watched, and sometimes it is thought prudent to exterminate them. All the important personages of the kingdom—patriarchs of the most powerful kinship groups, civil and military chiefs, great magicians and diviners—usually reside at court. The king asks their advice and charges them with executing his orders and giving judgment in his name as necessity requires.

Administering the Kingdom

Another category of rulers is delegated to administer the territory. When the territory over which the government has domain is too extensive to be directly administered by the monarch and his court, the kingdom is divided into several regions, into which officials are sent to exercise the royal powers. Territorial administration is what distinguishes a chiefdom from a kingdom. A chiefdom is not too large to be governed from one center, while a kingdom is sufficiently extensive to require secondary centers of administration. The main function of this administration is fiscal: surplus products must be collected in the form of taxes in kind and unpaid services. For example, in Buganda a network of wide paths connecting the capital with the various provinces was maintained by a labor force requisitioned by local officials.

The final government institution is the armed force on which, in the last analysis, the whole political system rests, since this is the instrument of physical coercion. It is found in various forms: highly disciplined regiments formed with a view to wars of conquest, like those of the Zulus after Chaka's military reform; warrior bands of Masai, specializing in raiding expeditions; armies raised at the beginning of each reign in Rwanda; police forces everywhere, sometimes composed of henchmen whose chief virtue was blind loyalty.

Centralizing

Such is, schematically, the organization common to all centralized African kingdoms. It is far from being in a state of permanent equilibrium. Tensions and internal oppositions are always latent: royal power aims at stronger and stronger centralization, which is resisted by local powers trying to retain or increase their autonomy. Such oppositions are, of course, universal, but in Africa they take the form of conflict between the old, basic lineage principle and the stronger, but less deep-rooted territorial principle. Originally, the secondary centers of administration were nearly always villages under a system of patriarchal democracy. Forced to recognize the power of a foreign king, the village was subjected to tribute but usually kept its own authorities. Then the pressure was increased; the king sent officials to represent him. But soon these officials tried to pass on their positions to their heirs. The principle of hereditary succession is so much in accordance with African customs that it crops up at every opportunity. The monarch himself, as we have mentioned, bases his legitimacy on it. Thus, as late as the nineteenth century, even in the kingdoms that had achieved a high degree of centralization, centrifugal forces continued to act. As soon as a weaker king came into power the balance shifted in favor of the local lineages.

Moreover, not all political systems had become centralized states. The great empires of the southern savannas were composed of several political units that recognized the supremacy of one of them and paid tribute to it. This explains the fluidity of these empires, which disintegrated as fast as they were formed. Thus in the area in what is now Northeast Angola, south Zaïre and Zambia, several kingdoms arose in succession. We are beginning to uncover their history. The first kingdom in this area was inhabited by Luba, but the rulers belonged to another people, the Songe. After freeing themselves from Songe tutelage, the Luba in their turn founded what some historians call the Second Luba Empire, which extended its influence over a large part of what is now Katanga. In the seventeenth century their neighbors, the Lunda, in their turn founded a broad empire extending from the Kwango to Lake Moëro. Also, the Lunda subjugated the kingdoms of the Bemba and the Rotse (now in Zambia) and the chiefdom of the Ovimbundu (now in Angola) as well as several other small states in the area.

Thus in the domain of politics, and the relationship of coercion between rulers and ruled, Africanity is manifested in forms common to African societies in which economic surplus allows the formation of a ruling group. Everywhere the state is monarchical; the sovereign's authority is absolute over the territory in which he can exercise coercive force through his army or his police; the monarchy derives its legitimacy from hereditary succession and its sacredness from the connection it establishes between the people and the vital forces for which it is the channel. The governmental instruments are, besides the monarch, the court and the army and, where the chiefdom has been replaced by the kingdom, the territorial administration. The ruling group can devote all its energies to the specialized tasks of government only because the relative prosperity of the total society frees it from the necessity of participating in the production of subsistence goods and because it can dispose, unchallenged, of the surplus obtained from cultivators and pastoralists.

Being Endowed with the Splendor of Power

Even though he is only an intermediary in the sphere of the sacred, the monarch occupies an important place in it, and he wants his glory to be a sign and witness of this. The humblest of the gods' ministers in all religions are, as we know, not averse to pomp and gold. Neither are those who rank highest in the secular order. The kings who inseparably unite these two preeminences in their own person like their glory to shine high and brilliant. We find its reflection in the work of craftsmen and artists.

The men who cast the wonderful Benin bronzes and carved delicate ivories were forbidden, on pain of death, to work for anybody but the *oba*, the king. Most of their works exalt royal power and grandeur. In the fourteenth and fifteenth centuries they produced idealized heads of queens, though still in a restrained style reminiscent of that of Ife. Then in the sixteenth and seventeenth centuries, came wall plaques depicting the *oba* flanked by burly warriors and complex war scenes, reminders of the importance of power and of the man who wields it. Last, from the eighteenth century on, the abundance of metals imported from Europe by sea—these goods had previously come by caravan across the Sahara—is shown in the use of higher relief and luxuriant decoration and the inclusion of many symbols of power. Alongside this court art there was a body of art in wood, practiced by the peasant population that was subject to the authority of the *oba* and the city-state of Benin. Thus, in the same society, we find a metal-wood dichotomy in aesthetic production corresponding to the ruler-subject dichotomy.*

In the kingdom of Dahomey, the unbaked clay bas-reliefs of Abomey palace recall the great military feats of the dynasty. For war history comes into being along with monarchies. In the centralized kingdoms of the east, where the pastoral tradition remained alien to the visual arts, the great events of each reign were celebrated in poetry and song.

Entering into History

The conceptual nature of African sculpture is not suited to portraiture. Nevertheless, Kuba artists succeeded in individualizing the statues of their kings: they can be identified by a symbol in high-relief on the pedestal representing one of the most characteristic deeds of his reign. A little, carved checkerboard enables us to recognize Shamba Bolongongo (who reigned around 1600-20): he introduced the game of *lela* to cure his people of a passion for much less innocent games of chance. An anvil characterizes Bope Pelenge (about 1800) because this king was a famous metal smith. A slave girl is the sign of Mikope Mbula (1810 to 1840): he repealed the ban on marriage between nobles and slaves.†

From the sixteenth century on, there became known in Europe statues in the round carved in soft stone by artists of the kingdom of Kongo. Despite their small size (12 to 20 inches in height), these sculptures are impressive in their monumentality, their high relief and their asymmetrical movement, all very rare

---

* William Fagg and Herbert List, *Nigerian Images: The Splendor of African Sculpture*. Praeger, New York, 1963.

† Frans M. Olbrechts, *Les Arts plastiques du Congo belge*. Erasme, Brussels, 1959.

in African statuary. These intensely alive figures are representations of chiefs. Their rank can be recognized by the headdress decorated with stylized leopard claws. Here, too, the artist is in the service of the rulers.*

The object most directly associated with political power is the scepter, the chief's staff or the rod of office. It is also an art object, for we see in it a concern for form over and above its use, which is to show publicly that the bearer holds or represents political authority. To achieve this aim, a staff marked with insignia would suffice. The scepters we admire in the kingdoms of Kongo, Dahomey, Luba, Songe and many other African monarchies are richly and delicately decorated. Sometimes they take the form of common tools such as the axe or adze, but, unlike these, they are ornamented and so become valuable and prestigious objects.†

If the beautiful is the splendor of the true, as Thomas Aquinas said, it is also the splendor of power. In Africa, art is closely linked with two essential themes of Africanity: ancestors and kings. In the most literal sense of the term, it gives shape to the relationship between man and his ancestors. Regarding power, artistic expression is involved in a more complex situation.

Being a Professional Craftsman

In societies with rulers, and therefore, with an economic surplus, the artist or artisan—there is no need to distinguish between them in this context—becomes a specialist who may devote if not all, at least much of his energies to his craft. The carvers of ancestor figures in village societies are also specialists in the sense that since they show greater competence than ordinary men they are more often asked to make statues for less talented neighbors. But because the group is small and its productivity low, they cannot make a living as craftsmen. However, in larger, wealthier societies the artisan has the opportunity to become a professional and live by practicing his trade.

* R. Verly, Les Mintadi. Zaïre, Brussels, 1955.
† Alexandre Adande, Les Récades des rois du Dahomey. I.F.A.N., Dakar, 1962.

Signs of professionalism first appear in more perfected tools and refined techniques. For example, Ife and Benin artists used the long, difficult lost wax process to make their famous bronze (copper and tin) or brass (copper and zinc) statues. The process is as follows. A wax model about three-quarters of an inch thick is made; in the top (according to the angle at which it is set) a number of wax tubes are inserted; the model is covered inside and out with damp, fire-proof clay, the outside layer being very thick to make the whole very strong; sometimes iron spikes are used to further strengthen it. When the clay is dry, it is heated; this melts the wax model leaving an empty space between the kernel and the outside into which molten metal is poured. At Ife, the head was placed so that the poured brass would cover the face first and its delicate modeling would stand the best chance of accurate rendering as air and loose bits of clay came out through the tubes left open at the back. Faults in casting were corrected in the same way; the repair was first made with clay-coated wax, which was melted and then replaced by molten metal.* These elaborate techniques give the pieces the finish that usually distinguishes professional from amateur work.

The anonymity of popular art gives way, at least sometimes, to the fame of a school. Thus with the Luba a school of wood carvers could be identified by the works it produced: stools supported by caryatids and Atlas figures. From the stylistic homogeneity and the aesthetic value of this series we can assume that they came from the same center, Buli. In Yoruba country certain master carvers won a great reputation and their works were sought after. At the beginning of the twentieth century Olowe of Ise, Agbonbiofe of Efon-Alaye and Bamgboye of Odo-Owa may be mentioned. Bamgboye was still alive in 1963. Agbonbiofe died about 1940 and Olowe, trained in the great center of sculpture of Efon-Alaye, left for Ise, where he entered the king's service. He developed a style of his own and died, famous, in 1938.†

* Léon Underwood, *Bronzes of West Africa*. Tiranti, London, 1949.
† Fagg and List, op. cit., pp. 83-85.

Olowe "entered the king's service." This direct dependence on power is customary for the professional artist living in state societies. It is not surprising that in these circumstances court art has produced so many royal effigies, scepters, thrones and representations glorifying the monarch. The professional artist could live only through his connection with political power. External trade is usually the rulers' prerogative: only they can obtain imported metals; only they have at their disposal enough consumer goods to support craftsmen and last, they insist on exclusive possession of rare and prestigious objects. In this way the firm trinity of art, power and wealth is formed.

The rulers were also the wealthy. However, an analysis of art enables us to distinguish between the two values wealth and power. Certain objects, certain features express one value rather than the other. We have just mentioned those that suggest majesty, strength and glory. Those catering to the taste for luxury and high living are made of rare and expensive materials: gold and ivory, bronze and valuable hardwoods; their function is to make their owner's daily life agreeable while showing his refinement and prosperity. The Kuba, for example, have goblets in the form of heads, cosmetic containers, head-rests, pipes, stools and raffia-embroidered cloth. The ostentatious nature of these objects is shown by an abundant, or even over-abundant, ornamentation of the entire surface.

Producing Folk Art

Not all African art exalts the wealth and power of the dominant minority. In addition to court art there is another kind. It uses iron and ordinary woods; its lines and mass are simple; it is roughly and ruggedly made: the marks of the adze and knife are not concealed by skilful polishing; it is sometimes clumsy and awkward and nearly always lively and strong. This is the art of the masks through which the gods can take material form and communicate with men. This is also the art of religious or magical statues, well-balanced weapons, graceful pots. Since we are speaking of art, not of craftsmanship, we do not include all such objects. They are often merely utilitarian, even the masks, yet many of them display a feeling for form that goes beyond their immediate significance. It is in this folk art that we find the popular, collective characteristics often attributed to African art. It does, of course, come from the people and is not imposed from above, but only one artistic stream can be regarded in this way. Not all African art is folk art.

Hewing Wood and Drawing Water

Rulers and ruled are unequal. This type of inequality is widespread in Africa and elsewhere: societies lacking state structure are a minority in the world. There is another social hierarchy, less universal but very important, for it has a profound influence on the personality of those who live within it. This is the division of a society into castes or classes.

Life in a stratified society provides a very special experience of human relationships. In two-caste societies—the kingdoms of the Great Lakes region, with a peasant majority and a minority of warrior herdsmen—the lower-caste man knows that irrespective of any personal qualities he may have individually inherited or achieved by his own efforts he will always be in a position inferior to that of any aristocrat, whatever personal deficiencies the latter may have. He knows that in any social relationship membership in different castes is the primary factor of which both parties are always aware and which will determine their respective behavior, especially if they do not know each other in any other context. The peasant knows that he must be respectful, not contradict, not refuse what is asked of him even if he cannot or does not want to do it, and especially he must not risk a conflict, for the rights of the aristocracy take precedence over his own. He also knows that the gap between the castes cannot be crossed by himself, his children, his relatives or his friends. When a social stratum relives this experience in each generation, it cannot fail to gradually develop the type of personality that enables a person best to adapt to the situation. Thus the commoners become dependent, a little servile, cunning, rather unsure of themselves, while the aristocrat will be authoritarian, self-assured, conscious of his superiority. The colonial relationship, which all African societies were later to know, is essentially a relationship of this type: in a colonial territory the European minority and the African majority are two castes.

It seems that a situation of social inequality is not easily accepted. It is often said that the idea of equality was introduced into Africa by the Europeans. It is true that this idea is part of Western tradition, but it did exist in Africa before the Europeans arrived. The proof of this is that the upper castes have felt the need to justify inequality, that certain proverbs and fables repeated among the peasants reveal their discontent, that the history of several attempted rebellions has come down to us.

The usual African justification for caste systems consists essentially in presenting them as part of the natural order of things and therefore unchangeable. Myths express this idea in symbols. The general schema is as follows: the ancestors of the two castes were brothers (and the ancestor of the lower caste is often the older); their father puts them to a test; through disobedience, foolishness, laziness or gluttony, the peasant ancestor fails while his brother, by his courage, shrewdness and skill, succeeds brilliantly; having thus proved his leadership qualities, the aristocrat ancestor wins the right to rule over his brother. Some men are made to command and others to be hewers of wood and drawers of water for the former. The Africans did not wait for the Europeans to discover equality nor to justify the natural rights of elites to command.

Fixing Inequalities

The parallel goes even further. The dominant caste emphasizes the differences between itself and the lower caste, and especially the innate, therefore unchangeable, differences. Stereotypes are created. In Rwanda, a caste society, the image the aristocrats have constructed of the peasants is amazingly similar to that held of Africans in general by the white colonists: impulsive, lacking a sense of responsibility, not very intelligent, incapable of concentrating on a long-term task and unable to resist the attraction of immediate pleasure.

To mark these distances, social segregation is practiced. The castes do not eat together, enjoy entertainment together or marry across caste lines. The elite and the masses do not enjoy the same judicial status. Cattle ownership is reserved for the aristocracy, and the castes have different tribunals.

In principle there is no social mobility. Actually there is some, for no society can completely suppress it; members of the aristocracy may be declassed by poverty; peasants may get rich. It is better to recognize these facts and regularize them by "naturalization." Thus the rich peasant who has managed to obtain cattle will marry the daughter of an aristocrat of modest means; one or two generations later their descendants will be regarded as belonging to the dominant group. But such cases have been exceptional.

A similar system of castes is seen in the Great Lakes societies. In the nineteenth century all the castes were not present in all the societies. But stratification was rigid enough so the horizontal divisions could be called castes, that is, closed social strata to which one can be admitted only by birth; classes, on the other hand, are open strata.

The caste societies of East Africa originated in conquest. Nomadic herders of long-horned cows settled in regions already occupied by farmers, who apparently lived in lineage-based village societies or in small chiefdoms. Superior weapons and the prestige of wealth in cattle enabled the herders to impose first their presence, then their domination and finally their complete overlordship. They formed total societies in which the two levels definitely froze the conquest situation.

The aristocracy did not content itself with social precedence and other non-material satisfactions. The upper caste enjoyed a privileged position economically. What physical control procured crudely and directly for the rulers through taxes, social pressure procured subtly and indirectly for the aristocratic caste. The colonial administration representing the power of the home country levied taxes and conscripted unpaid labor by coercion; but the whole colonial caste—businessmen, agents of industrial enterprises, officials of specialized services, agricultural and industrial settlers—enjoyed a very high standard of living the cost of which was ultimately borne by the African population. The channels through which this colonial prosperity was fed formed a complex network that was not immediately apparent.

Existing for Others

In societies where slavery existed, slaves formed the social stratum that suffered the greatest economic exploitation. Most often prisoners of war, slaves were of foreign origin. It is often stressed that African slavery, which was most widespread in the societies of the Sudan savanna and the Benin Gulf, was a domestic institution: the slave lived with the family group and after a few generations was absorbed into it, his standard of living being hardly inferior to that of his masters. It is true that except in a few cases—in Dahomey and Bamum societies, for example—slavery of the type known in the ancient classical world did not exist: there were no great plantations or workshops using the labor of anonymous masses. However, even when they were treated kindly, these men and women were entirely at the disposal of their masters. Everything they produced—labor, and children—belonged entirely to their masters; they were inherited; they were tools of production. Of course they were fed, supported and even treated well. Was not this how any normal stock-raiser treated his livestock?

In Africa the slave was certainly a slave: the property of another person. But he was a member of his owner's household and could hope for formal emancipation, if not for himself then at least for his descendants; he was thus exploited only to a moderate degree. We must remember that economic surplus, important as it was in these societies, did not have the same meaning as in a monetary economy, and it had still less meaning than in a capitalist economy. Agricultural products were used to support a string of dependents and to exchange for other goods. Of course, powerful men liked to increase the number of their followers, but this increase could be achieved only gradually and up to a certain point. They also liked to enjoy consumer goods obtained by trade, but, except in the Sudan societies, the kingdoms of the Gulf of Guinea and the mouth of the Congo, a market economy was only slightly developed. It is hard for us to imagine these conditions limiting the utilization of an agricultural surplus, so used are we to the possibility of savings and investment that money provides, so convinced that the profit motive is enough in itself and so accustomed to living in a world where the ever-growing overabundance of desirable goods always exceeds the possibilities of their acquisition. The absence of these economic stimuli in traditional Africa explains why the slave system did not generate as much abuse as elsewhere.

But it began to do so when Arab and European traffickers made slaves an object of trade, that is, something that could be exchanged for imported goods. For his owner, the slave was no longer an instrument that produced an agricultural surplus but a piece of merchandise that, like ivory, gold or valuable timber, had a market value. To obtain slaves for European slave traders, the coastal groups made more and more military expeditions; these became very murderous, for something much more important than hitherto was at stake in warfare. People struggled to defend themselves against those who wanted to take captives to sell to slavers. It is highly probable that the scope and cruelty of the bloody customs reported by nineteenth-century travelers in the Gulf of Guinea kingdoms—executions and sacrifices— were indirect consequences of the new meaning of slavery: life can hardly be respected when people seek to capture men in order to sell them in lands across the ocean, lands they do not always reach and from which they never return.

Serving the Lord

Free men of the lower stratum were not subjected to such direct exploitation as were slaves. But the upper stratum still obtained important economic advantages from them. How was this?

Among the forms of social organization that made such a situation possible, an especially effective and well-balanced institution is the feudal relationship as it existed in certain stratified kingdoms in the pastoral areas of the eastern highlands. The relationship was formed in this way: a peasant of the lower, agricultural caste would ask a warrior herdsman to allow him to become his dependent, "his man." If the aristocrat accepted this homage, he would give the peasant a cow. This transfer of a head of cattle—a transfer not of ownership but only of possession—was the sign and proof of the agreement between the two men. This agreement gave rise to obligations on both sides. The peasant owed his lord regular gifts—for example, hampers of sorghum and haricots or large pots of banana beer—and donations of labor—for example, building and repairing houses, herding cattle or transporting goods; the lord granted the peasant the usufruct of the cow entrusted to him—milk and male calves—but retained actual ownership of the original cow and her female calves.

This appears to be a voluntary contract of exchange of economic benefits between two parties. Actually it was a one-sided contract, for the lord determined the size of his dependent's donations, and if the peasant complained they were too large, he risked bringing serious trouble upon himself; a cow's production of milk was low and unreliable; at any time the lord could take his cattle back. The reason the peasant sought feudal dependence was not for economic advantages but because protection by a member of the upper caste was necessary for his safety. To be defended against abuse of the considerable social power of any aristocrat, the commoner had to be in a position to oppose him with a social power of the same order. Through the bond of personal dependence he identified himself with the social power of his lord, a peer of the other aristocrats.

Feudalism is one of the mechanisms by which the upper caste obtained agricultural goods without having to produce them by work or exchange equivalent pastoral products for them. There are various indirect ways of transforming the weight of social superiority into material benefit. Feudalism is one of the most elegant.

Thus the traditional societies of Africa were not all equalitarian. The heterogeneity resulting from the conquest of one people by another or from the differentiation of subsistence techniques often crystallized into a hierarchical structure. There was equality in hunters' camps, in bands of nomadic warrior herdsmen, in agricultural villages and in blacksmiths' associations, but whenever two of these groups co-existed within the same global society the division apparently tended to become horizontal rather than vertical. And the social superiority of one group tended to be immediately expressed by privileged access to goods. In the realm of organization of human relationships, Africanity also includes structures of inequality and exploitation: hierarchical strata, slavery and feudalism.

Structuring the African Heritage

Seeking to specify the content of Africanity we have surveyed the major aspects of culture, the universal categories of all civilizations: kinship, marriage and the family; the spatial organization and social control of the community; the socialization of the young by their upbringing and education, philosophical conceptions and world view; government and social stratification; religion and magic; ritual and art. In unfurling this panoramic view, institutions and ideas common to all African societies, or the great majority of them, have stood out in each category. Thus with regard to marriage, African marriage has a look peculiar to itself: it is an alliance between two lineages rather than the union of two individuals; bride wealth is an essential element of it, and it is polygynous. Africanity is not an abstract concept divorced from reality; it has a positive, rich, material content.

This content is illuminated and elucidated to some degree when set against two other universal categories, techniques and economy. Some brief and simplified analyses—the only ones possible within the restricted limits of this book—have shown how the material foundation of a society (its system of production and distribution of goods) always limits the possibility of other cultural divisions and sometimes determines them. These reflections of basic structures by the various aspects of a civilization follow complex laws that are still far from being elucidated. But the connections we have sketched at least show that the contents of Africanity are not incomprehensible facts, since they are continuous with technico-economic realities. Thus the low productivity of forest agriculture allows only small concentrations of population; after two or three generations, these normally consist of related families; hence the importance of descent in placing an individual in his society; this is reflected in the concept of life-force coming from an ancestor; this is the basis of the patriarch's authority and is expressed in the ritual of ancestor worship in which ancestors are represented by statues that suggest the fertility of the lineage.

Within Africanity itself, a certain duality is revealed. On the one hand, there are socially homogeneous village societies and patriarchal and equalitarian democracies in which kinship is the dominant principle of the organization of human relationships and in which the art of carving statues and masks may be called a folk art; on the other hand, there are chiefdoms and kingdoms ruled by a group that exercises control in the name of a sacred monarch, and these are territorially based societies in which various forms of privilege and exploitation may be discerned and in which there developed a court art created by professionals. This does not, however, break the unity of Africanity, for in the chiefdoms there are villages, in state territories there are lineages and, not far from the courts, folk art flourishes. Again we see the point of departure of this duality on the technico-economic level: precisely where techniques and environment make an agricultural surplus possible.

The head of a maternity statue, Lulua tribe. Kasai province, Zaïre (Musée Royal d'Afrique Centrale, Tervuren, Belgium)

A Wooden mask from the Kuba region, Zaïre. Made c. 1950

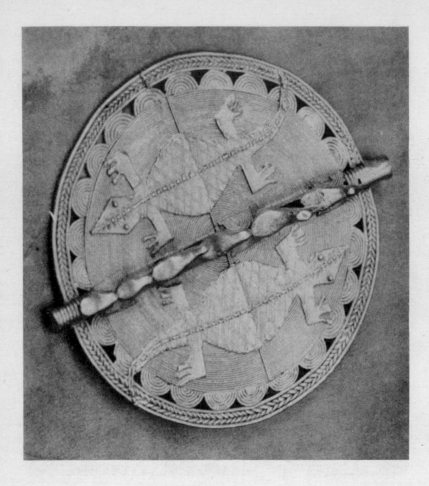

A gold ornament. Baule, Ivory Coast

Concrete sculpture in a public square. Bouaké, Ivory Coast

Pottery market. Bouaké, Ivory Coast

A painting by Joseph Kabongo. Lubumbashi, Republic of Zaïre

A Harrist church. Harris was a prophet who founded a religious movement in West Africa at the beginning of this century. The movement was inspired by Christianity but incorporated many traditional religious practices. Bregbo, Ivory Coast

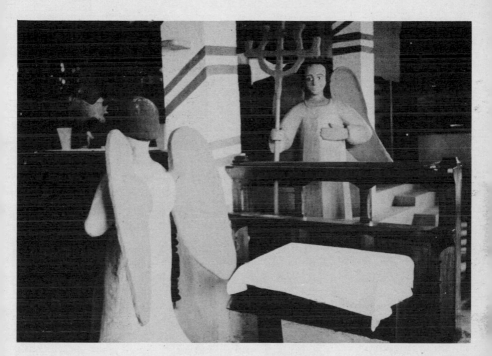

Inside another Harrist church. Mbaton, Ivory Coast

The Danish fort of Accra, built in the eighteenth century by the Danish merchants. Accra, Ghana

Fort-Jesus in Mombasa, Kenya. Built by the Portuguese in the sixteenth century, it was later used as a prison

View of the old city of Kano, Nigeria

PROSPECTS FOR
AFRICANITY

Of the four sources of Africanity we have discussed—type of subsistence technique, intense cultural diffusion in sub-Saharan Africa, isolation of the interior of the continent, entry into the outside world in the age of industry—only the first three have affected the nature of the contents briefly described in the third chapter: the heritage of traditional Africa. It is not that the fourth source, the opening up of Africa to the world, did not operate: it changed the face of Africa. Its strength, its suddenness, its extent were so great that its contributions have not yet been digested, assimilated or africanized. Which of its elements will be definitely integrated into Africanity? Because the answer to this question is uncertain, we did not want to include in the same picture the solid traditional elements of Africanity and its recent enrichments that are not yet stabilized.

It was during the period of combined economic and political dependence under the colonial regime that industrial techniques and their cultural effects invaded Africa. Thus all the new elements were imposed, but the African peoples could not, at least not openly, choose, interpret and adapt. Even in the sphere of religion the Africans were denied the right to assimilate Christianity in their own way. And yet, is not the Western, twentieth-century Christianity that was preached to them itself a syncretism of which the Judaic sources had often been re-interpreted in the course of two millenia in the light of other cultural heritages—those of the Greeks, the Romans, the Franks and the Germans, the peasants and clerics of the Middle Ages, the intellectuals of the Renaissance, the aristocrats of the *ancien régime*, the bourgeois and so on? Yet a colonial sociologist wrote forty years ago that the conversion of the Africans was not "worthy of the name" since, understanding Christianity in their own cultural perspective, they corrupted and distorted it*

Thus we must wait until politically independent states emerge before we can try to specify which foreign contributions will be taken in Africa and in what way.

Struggling Together

The movements to end colonization that have occurred up to now have been relatively peaceful (it is to be feared that those yet to come—in Angola, Mozambique, Rhodesia and South Africa—will not be). The new political institutions were developed by the colonial governments before they left. They were, of course, influenced by the public law of the home countries, and thus the different constitutions came into being, the last legacy of the "civilizers." The new states set up republics (except for Burundi and Swaziland, which became kingdoms, and Lesotho, which is a state-chiefdom), usually with a parliamentary government in which the chief of state is distinct from the head of the government. These institutions presuppose the existence of more than one party and, in the Anglo-Saxon view, more precisely two parties: the majority party as the government and the minority party as the parliamentary opposition that acts as a check on the government and hopes to supersede it if free elections give it a majority of votes.

Actually, four or five years after these constitutions took effect, political life did not develop in the way intended. A presidential system in which the head of state himself assumes the

* René Maunier, *Sociologie coloniale.* Domat-Montchrestien, Paris, 1932, pp. 158-59.

direction of the executive has been substituted for the parliamentary system; parliament, when it is authorized to sit, contents itself with passing legislation and voting budgets. The man who thus concentrates very extensive powers in his own hands is a respected, even charismatic, leader of the struggle against colonialism. The presidential system is not characteristic of Africa; it proved itself in the United States. But it is significant that in spite of their constitutions the African states have turned in this direction. Moreover, in Africa the presidential system has taken on its own coloration: it is reinterpreted in the light of traditional political conceptions. Léopold Senghor, president of Senegal, believes that it expresses the spirit of African philosophy. "The president," he said in one of his speeches, "personifies the nation as the old time monarch personified 'his' people. The masses make no mistake; they speak of the 'reign' of Modibo Keita, Sekou Touré or Houphouet-Boigny, in whom they see above all the man chosen by God through the people."*

The presidential regime is accompanied and reinforced in Africa by a one-party system. Here too we are reminded of certain political elements of traditional Africanity: the king's henchmen who, with other subgroups, constitute the governmental apparatus, and the rule of unanimity which, when the palaver is over, does not allow an opposition party to survive. This continuity with the past may perhaps explain the ease with which the one-party system was adopted but not the fact that it seems to have been inevitable everywhere.

The one-party system arose from other legacies of colonization: the arbitrariness of territorial frontiers, the authoritarianism of administrations and the economic stagnation of African populations.

The political units that became independent about 1960 were colonial territories the frontiers of which had been established by European colonial offices around 1885. When the boundaries

* Léopold Sédar Senghor, *Democracy and Socialism* (lecture delivered at the University of Ibadan, April 10, 1964), University ("roneo." print), Ibadan, p. 11.

of spheres of influence were drawn on maps, the diplomats took no account of the frontiers of African kingdoms or traditional cultural and linguistic areas; often they knew nothing about the physical layout of the territory. For example, at the end of the nineteenth century the British, German and Belgian governments quarreled for nearly twenty years over the possession of "Mfumbiro," near Lake Kivu. Things went a long way, for in 1909 Belgian and British troops were on the point of fighting over Mfumbiro. The home governments, however, did not know what Mfumbiro was (a mountain? a volcanic mass? a region?) nor why it was important. (It was, in fact, a series of eight volcanoes, mostly south of 1° latitude south and west of the 30th meridian; now these volcanoes are usually called the Virunga mountains.)

Even on the maps, frontier lines were uncertain or deceptive. In 1884–5, over a ten-month period, King Leopold of Belgium concluded one agreement with Germany and another with France and made a declaration of neutrality as sovereign of the independent state of the Congo. A map of the frontiers of the new state went with each of the diplomatic statements. The line of the eastern boundary of the Congo was different on each of the three maps!* These artificial dissections always put together in the same colony units that were traditionally very different and often separated other units into two or three parts. Thus the great traditional kingdom of Kongo found itself divided between Portuguese Angola, the Belgian Congo and the French Middle Congo.

Awakening the National Consciousness

This arbitrary formation of colonial territories was not favorable for the emergence of a national sentiment based on them. There were also other, more significant obstacles, the most important being that the territories were colonies, that is, oppressive organizations imposed by foreigners. How could the Africans

* Roger W. Louis, *Rwanda-Urundi 1884-1919*. Clarendon Press, Oxford, 1963, pp. 52-91.

have positive feelings toward them? Besides, the colonial powers, careful to "divide and rule," supported old loyalties and discouraged any broad-based patriotism: it would have become a social force potentially dangerous to their domination. Lord Lugard's doctrine of indirect rule, prescribing colonial government through the mediation of traditional authorities, which are thus compromised and integrated into the colonial administration, is the clearest example of this position. Thus, when decolonization came, African leaders found themselves at the head of states in which national consciousness hardly existed. Patrice Lumumba's desperate struggle to awaken a feeling of Congolese nationalism in his fellow-countrymen is well known. In countries where national identity is so weakly felt, party rivalry, especially when the parties are based on old tribal or regional memberships, may threaten the very existence of the national community and hence of the state. Avoidance of this danger is one of the functions of the one-party system.

The political immaturity of the citizens of Western countries has often been deplored. This, it is said, is why the delicate mechanisms of parliamentary democracy cannot work well. Political maturity is even less evident in the young African nations. Of course, village democracy has developed a sense of responsibility to the community. But three-quarters of a century of colonial rule had seriously blunted it. (Seventy-five years is a short time in the life of a society, but a long time in an individual's.) All the colonial administrations were authoritarian. The governor's powers were entrusted to him by the home government, and he was accountable only to it. Moreover, the colonial administration were more military than civil in appearance. Officials wore uniforms, exercised police powers and often were required to practice the daily ritual of saluting the flag. The people they governed were subjects, not citizens. Only toward the end of the colonial period was this authoritarianism modified by the creation of advisory assemblies at various levels of the hierarchy. These moves in the direction of participation in the administration of public affairs were very modest. African executive bodies with power to make decisions were rarely set up, and when they were, it was only in situations where the process of decolonization was already under way. In these circumstances it is not surprising that the political form of parliamentary democracy had some trouble in developing in the newly independent states.

Conquering Poverty

However, the most important factor that led some African countries toward a concentration of power characteristic of single-party presidential rule was the demands of the economy. This point requires some explanation.

Colonization did not bring advanced industrial technology to all the African territories. So far as very low wages made it possible, many enterprises preferred to employ a very large labor force rather than rationalize and mechanize its production. In the short run this was more profitable. This was the case not only on the plantations but also in mining: some huge tin and gold operations used hand methods exclusively. In these areas, of course, the African population did not enjoy a high standard of living. But even in fortunate areas where rich lodes were exploited by powerful modern industrial complexes—for example, in the copper belt of Northern Rhodesia (now Zambia) and Katanga—the people as well were in that inferior economic situation called underdevelopment. Underdevelopment is a relative quality; it is measured by the standard of living, that is the average income, of the population of industrialized countries of North America, Western Europe and the Soviet Union. International proprieties suggest the use of this term (or still better "in process of development"), which actually means, simply, poverty.

The paradox of the co-existence of poverty and advanced industrial development in certain parts of Africa is explained by their economic dependence. Because they were colonies, these areas were placed in a subordinate position in a broader system outside their control. Colonial enterprises used foreign capital and had foreign boards of directors, management personnel and high-level technical experts. The high profits were due to the very low wage levels (compared with those of comparable industrial workers in Western Europe and North America), to specialization in the most profitable enterprises (mining of valuable materials) and to comparatively low income taxes. Moreover, these high profits were mostly taken out of the country rather than reinvested locally in processing industries that, while less profitable, are necessary for balanced economic development. Thus in spite of their important local contributions in labor and raw materials, the colonial territories remained underdeveloped.

The end of political colonization did not change this economic structure of dependence: the new states that wanted to liberate themselves and overcome poverty had to make a considerable effort. They had little monetary wealth, few technicians and trained management personnel. As a starting point they have (though not always) exploitable raw materials, the beginning of an industrial infrastructure and men. It is men who will have to prime the pump by working without the immediate benefit of a noticeable rise in their standard of living, since a large part of the wealth produced by their labor has to be invested in equipment. Economic aid, even if substantial and "disinterested," cannot overcome the need for austerity.

Some of the new nations that have followed this path feel that a highly structured party organized in cells and operating even in the smallest villages, is needed to rally the entire population to mobilize all its energies and make it understand a development program that requires immediate sacrifices in face of distant rewards. Obviously such a party can be *one* party only.

Other new nations do not seem to be striving to reorient the colonial economic structure, and they are willing or obliged to accommodate themselves to that state of economic dependence which is called neo-colonialism. But Western-type parliamentary democracy does not fare any better with them. Here the one party is only nominally a people's party; its function is that of the bands of faithful henchmen of the former kingdoms: to protect the power and privileges of a ruling group. However, it would be particularly hypocritical to work up a righteous indignation about this state of affairs. Although African political institutions of yesterday and today have their own special features, they also display characteristics common to all governments. The statement that "power corrupts" was not made with reference to Africa. This remark has, unfortunately, a universal application rarely achieved in comparative sociology.

Asking ourselves whether the presidential form of government and the one-party system may be included in the newly acquired content of Africanity, we found that this apparently simple question involved many threads stretching backward and forward. We must remember the arbitrary partition of Africa, the nature of colonial administration, the new patriotism, underdevelopment and neo-colonialism. This complexity of connections and influences makes us very wary of drawing conclusions. Presidential government and the one-party system express in a modern context certain traditional constants and answer certain pressing needs of new nations. Since these problems—the development of national consciousness and the struggle against poverty—will not be solved in the immediate future, the leadership of one man and one party will remain an important element in African political life for rather a long time.

Progressing

When European expansion in Africa was at its height in the thirties, an expert in "colonial studies" remarked with some surprise that aspiration to independence is based for the Blacks —"who would believe it!" he wrote—on the idea of progress, while for other "exotic" peoples, in particular the Arabs, it is based on a desire for restoration of, or a return to, the past.*
We are less astonished by this trend toward progress: we have already discerned it in the many cultural borrowings that have occurred among traditional African societies. Once colonization had opened the door to some outside influences, the Africans adopted certain new elements with enthusiasm and not always those that had been imposed or pressed upon them. Among these elements were knowledge and techniques. In a few in-

* Maunier, op. cit., pp. 77-78.

'stances certain societies refused these values; these cases of obstinate conservatism—such as that of the Suk of Kenya—are very rare.*

These two values were and are eagerly sought after because they seemed to the Africans to lead to a better life. In this, the African viewpoint is very close to the Western. There is no African or Western Gandhi dreaming of a society in which people weave their clothes, till their fields and lead a simple, sober life directed to the search for peace and inner harmony through overcoming desire. Asceticism is no more African than Western.

As soon as colonizers opened schools, students flocked to them. Elementary education, all that was required for the needs of colonization, was made available. This did not satisfy the Africans. They demanded secondary schools, then access to universities, either abroad or in establishments set up in the colonial territories. They obtained something of what they wanted, most in French and British Africa, less in Belgian Africa and still less in Portuguese Africa. The important thing in the present discussion is to stress this African thirst for knowledge. Under the colonial regime the Africans showed their opposition in many spheres by passive resistance, yet they actively welcomed all kinds of teaching. For school learning of the European type was the main road, often the only one, by which an individual could improve his social situation; this is still true in independent Africa. Moreover, it is an indispensable condition for the development of the national collectivity.

Ever since their first contact with the Whites, the Africans admired their power over the physical environment. More than mastery over men, they envied that mastery over things that achieved a high standard of living with apparent ease. With the installation of industrial enterprises and great commercial plantations they saw how modern production techniques created wealth. But, with such a niggardly share of the benefits that their labor played so large a part in producing, the Africans felt

* Harold K. Schneider, "Pakot Resistance to Change." *Continuity and Change in African Cultures*, op. cit., pp. 144-67.

themselves constantly frustrated in the colonial period. Kept on the fringe of the technical and economic organization, the African workers could never effect their own mechanized production of goods from raw material. The peasant majority, still using their ancient agricultural methods were at an even greater disadvantage. All, however, were fully agreed on the value of efficiency. Africans certainly did not prefer to use a picturesque, fragile pottery container when an aluminum pot was available. Neither did they hesitate to have recourse to the most up-to-date medicines to treat diseases.

While other non-literate populations—the Indians on reservations in North America or the Indians of Latin America, for example—seem to have been traumatized by their contact with industrial civilization, the Africans welcomed two essential aspects of that civilization with an eagerness that reveals great self-confidence. This selective receptivity to innovation seems to be a constant factor in Africanity.

Westernizing or Universalizing

What Africa wants to adopt—knowledge obtained from the written word, technique, and efficiency—was, to a degree, brought before the eleventh century by the Arabs, the Maghrebins and the Portuguese and then, to a much greater degree, during the colonial period by the Europeans on whom it was politically dependent. But what the European countries gave to Africa, in any case only incompletely, was not the heritage of a few nations; it was the common property of humanity. We Westerners are accustomed to seeing ourselves rather smugly as the proprietors of science and technology. But a great part of "our" science and technology was invented elsewhere (for a start, the alphabet in Southwest Asia about 1000 B.C.; mathematics in ancient Greece; paper in China in the first century of our era.) The techniques that originated in Western European societies (such as the many industrial processes used for the first time in nineteenth-century Britain) have, rightly enough, already passed into the common heritage of twentieth-century humanity. That is why Africa is universalizing rather than westernizing.

Furthermore, independence has opened up for Africa avenues of communication with the world other than those of the European countries of the colonial period. Americans, Soviets, Chinese, Czechs and Israelis are bringing to Africa the practical knowledge and techniques of production and organization that it asks for.

We stress the supranational nature of Africa's borrowings because the formation of a heritage held in common by all the peoples of the world is a new phenomenon. For the first time in history the multiplicity, intensity and speed of communication of ideas, things and people are such that a world civilization is in the process of formation. Science and techniques are rightly classed as the sectors in which this process is going furthest and fastest. Today all societies draw deeply on this common fund. Thus the African nations that are doing the same need not worry about following in the wake of the former colonial powers.

Retaining Identity

Desiring material progress, Africa means to borrow what will lead to this, but Africa is resolved to retain its identity. That is, to reinterpret borrowings in harmony with traditional Africanity and, in some ways, to live within its own heritage without borrowing. This, we think, sums up the intentions of responsible African men of culture. They know that colonial alienation resides not only in political institutions and economic structures but also in ideas. They want to break definitively with the past but to remain faithful to it. Is such an undertaking viable? This is the whole problem of traditional Africanity in the world of today and tomorrow. Any thinking, any discussion of the arts, literature, philosophy, architecture or social and family life in contemporary Africa sooner or later encounters this problem.

We do not doubt that the ways of living, thinking, working, carrying on interpersonal relationships and making things that prevail in a society—in short, its culture—constitute an integrated whole or that the production of material goods plays a determining part in the integration of this whole. These are the two basic hypotheses that help interpret traditional civilizations. Let us apply them to the present situation.

No African country can at present be described by the enviable term "industrial society." However, agricultural production on the subsistence level in small family units belongs to yesterday's Africa. A considerable proportion of the population, still a minority but economically the most productive section, works in industrial manufacturing or extraction enterprises; in large-scale, sometimes even mechanized, plantations; in production for the international market; in large import and export businesses. Governments work out development plans, foreseeing the harnessing of powerful energy sources, the building of an important basic organization, the creating of industries. This is why we believe that after the civilizations of the bow, the clearings, the granaries, the spear, and the cities, the civilization of industry, that is, of industrial technique, has already begun in Africa.

Africans eagerly accept this orientation offered them by history. But will not these industrial techniques gradually influence all other aspects of the life of African societies and finally eliminate traditional Africanity?

Bending the Culture

Certainly the industrialization of a society has effects far beyond the technical level. Its repercussions can already be seen in such diverse spheres as habitat, kinship obligations, family and local authorities.

Africans used to live in villages. Except in the Sudan region and the coast of the Benin Gulf area, urban settlements were almost unknown. Industrially based societies are urban: to partake of the benefits of the city, enterprises congregate; their personnel must live near their place of work; schools, hospitals and other public institutions result from the influx of population and attract more people. In 1961 it was estimated that about ten per cent of the population of Africa lived in cities. Even more significant are the rate and speed of growth.*

This change of habitat completely alters everyday life. Even if he lives in a settlement of only a few tens of thousands of inhabitants, the African workman or wage-earner has a style of urban life very different from the life-style that developed among peasants, herders, craftsmen and hunters. Instead of building his house with the help of his lineage, he buys or rents it, or is granted the use of it by his employer or the municipality. In a village a new house can always be built when needed, in a town there is a constant housing problem and dwellings are overcrowded. In the country a family is assured of the greater part of its food by its own crops and livestock, in the town everything must be bought.

In an industrial society wages are earned, and their level is calculated on the basis of the needs of the individual or the household. But in addition, lineage solidarity continues to impose obligations from time to time: a brother coming to town to look for work needs help or a nephew or niece studying in town must be supported. In this new situation these kinship duties cannot be fully carried out because they are incompatible with the socioeconomic organization produced by industrial technology.

We have already spoken of the essential political and economic functions of the polygynous family in traditional African civilizations. These functions become superfluous when political offices are no longer hereditary and the agricultural unit of production is no longer the conjugal family. For the industrial worker whose only income is his wages the support of more than one wife could become a burden that few men have the means to carry.

The local authority of the village, whether it be the senior patriarch or the king's representative, can be exercised as a whole by just one man, because the administration of public affairs is relatively simple. In large towns resulting from the

* See the figures given in Maquet, *Civilizations of Black Africa*, op. cit., pp. 179-80.

industrialization of a society, administration has become so complex that it is impossible to lay responsibility for it on one man. It includes such diverse matters as the organization and management of schools, hospitals, medical services, water supply and electricity; the regulation of business and traffic; the maintenance of order in a large heterogeneous and mobile population in which the pressure of public opinion, so effective in villages where everybody knows everybody else, carries very little weight.

These few examples show how the introduction of industrial technology into a society affects, according to its requirements, aspects of culture that seem to have little connection with it. Will this process continue to its logical conclusion, which would be the uniformity of all the industrial civilizations of the world, whether they be African, Western, Asiatic or Soviet?

Preserving Africanity

This would probably be the case if industrial technology developed in a cultural vacuum. Men unmarked by any past experience would then create a society, a philosophy and an art based only on the requirements of a technology and the common experience of industrial labor. Fortunately this is not the case. Societies in the process of industrialization have different histories, and these past experiences, still living in the cultures they created, constitute forces that resist the changes brought by industrialization.

When people so desire—and in Africa it seems that they do—the living heritage of history can be maintained in certain spheres, because technical determinism is more negative than positive and because there is great flexibility in areas remote from material basis.

Technical determinism is negative in the sense that it precludes rather than imposes certain institutions or systems. Industrialization precludes living in villages, but it can quite as well fit in with a network of medium-size towns as with one or two enormous cities. A subsistence economy cannot for long co-exist in the same country with industrial development, but the latter can prosper just as well in an economic system of private capital as in the United States or in a system of collective ownership as in the Soviet Union. Tribal government and modern techniques are incompatible, but the latter can just as well accommodate a monarchy (Great Britain or Japan) as a republic (France or Italy). Common ownership of land is a traditional African legal form. If Africans want it, it may be maintained: individual private property is not indispensable to modern Africa.

The further we go from the technical foundation—if we may thus translate conceptual difference into spatial distance—the less influence it exerts, while the pressure of the past grows in strength. The conception of death is influenced much more by the cultural past than by a new technique of production. Ideas and attitudes slowly developed over many generations lead people to believe that there is personal survival after death, that death marks the loss of individuality in a universal reality or that death plunges the individual into nothingness. Art, though "a reflection of society," does not reflect social reality directly and immediately. Thus at the same time (1950), the main trends in painting in two great industrial complexes, Western Europe and the Soviet Union, were on the one hand nonfigurative and on the other the strictest naturalism.

This is the viewpoint from which we must look at the future of religions in Africa. It has often been said that the traditional religions have had their day and are no longer valid in modern Africa. But the traditional religion of the West, Christianity, and the traditional religion of the Arab world, Islam, also arose before industrialization. They correspond to a stage of society based on the kind of agriculture, craftsmanship and trade analogous to the civilization of cities in West Africa from the twelfth to the nineteenth centuries. Thus modern African societies are faced with two types of religion, imported monotheisms and indigenous cults, neither of which compels recognition more than the other: both arose in pre-industrial civilizations, but neither seems to be incompatible with the demands of modern development. The strangeness to us of the suggestion that the traditional cults are viable in the modern world is a proof of

Western ethnocentrism. For these religions have marked advantages. First, having been fashioned by innumerable generations of Africans, they express the specifically African way of relating to the gods. Second, they establish communication between man and the whole continuous reality of the world more directly than the "great monotheistic religions," which are at the same time more intellectual (being based on sacred texts) and more material (being expressed in heavy social structures). Third, not being founded on sacred books, and not being equipped with a priesthood to preserve orthodoxy, African religions are flexible and adaptable.

Making Civilizations More Alike

Thus in the upper levels of the superstructure—world views and religions—and in art and literature—Africanity can maintain itself if Africans so wish, for a time at least. For two mechanisms are operating that tend to make industrial societies more alike. The first is consistency. As we have shown, production techniques act negatively on other aspects of a culture and allow of several alternatives, especially in certain spheres. However, the effect of the environment on the individual and the group in the industrial period is far different from that on the hunter or the farmer. Just as their farmer ancestors gradually translated their existential experience into ideas, philosophies and art forms, the men who live after the Industrial Revolution will slowly develop a new vision of reality that corresponds effectively to their own experience. And gradually the mental constructs translating other experiences will become blurred. Thus the personification of natural forces and their manipulation by magic, which reflects man's experience of the resistance or even the hostility of the physical environment to a group with a simple technology, will give way to the conception of man's domination of the environment that is characteristic of a technical, well-developed urban culture. But of course these ripenings are slow.

The mechanism of diffusion through the media is much faster in the age of industry. Records, radio, cinema, illustrated magazines and air transport enable pictures, ideas, things and people to become known worldwide. Thus almost simultaneously people all over the world start wearing jeans; informal non-figurative paintings are done in Paris, New York and Tokyo, people dance to the same music wherever there are tape recorders, the same movies are shown wherever there are cinemas. This world culture, through the simple power of means of reproduction that yield cheaply huge numbers of copies of pictures, sounds and writings, weighs heavily on cultural specificity. The artist who shuts himself off in a local tradition now scarcely has an audience.

Through their contributions to this world culture, the various civilizations can also become universal. To a very high degree, the tradition of a particular society can henceforth enrich the common heritage of humanity. If swift, large-scale cultural diffusion gives rise to a fear of uniformity, it also awakens a great hope, the hope that the best and most original creations of various societies will be made available to all.

Enriching World Art

Africa did not only welcome technical progress and preserve its own originality; it also contributed to this collective enrichment. When we remember that Africa entered the world stream less than a century ago, and did so in the unfavorable circumstances of colonial regimes, its contribution is considerable.

It was made chiefly in the realm of the arts. The discovery of African sculpture about 1907 by the cubist painters of the Paris School guided their aesthetic orientation. What they were groping for had already been achieved in Africa: works that were not concerned with imitating visual impressions but that expressed the artist's own conception of an object or a person; work, that, like true sculpture, had an independent existence and the static, even rigid, nature of a sign. This convergence influenced Picasso and Braque and, through them, many other painters.[*]

* Daniel-Henry Kahnweiler, *Confessions esthétiques*, Gallimard, Paris, 1963, pp. 222-36.

Later, about 1925, African art was exalted by the surrealists. They thought they saw in it a direct, authentic and strange expression of the deep, non-rational regions of man's mind. In African statues they saw not so much the cultural content as the unconscious meaning and the dream content. This point of view is debatable: we do not think that African art is freer than other art of social rules and rational controls; it is only because they knew nothing of the cultural context that the surrealists endowed these works with exceptional freedom. These objects coming from unknown societies were strange and liberating only in Europe. Whether understood or misunderstood, African art has had considerable influence on Western painters and sculptors over the last half-century.

It has also had a more diffuse but no less strong influence on public taste. Gradually, through museums, exhibitions and art books, African forms are becoming familiar to the eye. They are appreciated and sought after, and so the aesthetic sensibility of the Western public has become enriched by the perception of a new world of forms.

More recently, traditional dance and music have come out of Africa. These two arts, always linked in African societies, are known from records, films and traveling companies. The best of them alter their material as little as possible to adapt to the time and space requirements of European and American performances and attempt to preserve the authenticity of movements and sounds. Thus the world benefits from these characteristic creations of Africanity.

On the level of popular culture, which reaches a much larger public, the African contribution is much older and more mixed, but still essential. The traditional music the slaves brought to the New World is one of the sources of Latin American rhythms and of jazz and prevails in dance music as much in the Soviet as in the Western world, as much in Asia as in Africa. For the circle is now closed: the music that is danced to in the bars of African industrial cities—the "high life" of the west coast cities —is directly inspired by Latin American dance music and jazz.

The verbal arts, which were very much alive throughout traditional Africa and especially brilliant among pastoralists,

are less easily diffused than the visual arts or music: oral literature must be translated. This task, only just begun, has already
produced some very beautiful poetry. Here again an older diffusion dates from the time of slavery: in the West Indies, in
Brazil and even in the United States, children are told African
stories that are so well integrated into American cultures that
those who repeat them do not know that they come from the
forests and savannas of Africa.

Contributing to the World Culture

It is significant that the contributions of traditional Africanity to
world culture are mainly in the realm of arts and letters. As is
exemplified by the relationship between Rome and Greece, this
is the only domain in which conquerors and masters allow themselves to be influenced by their subjects. For this reason we
may expect an increase in African influence in spheres other
than the arts, following the consolidation of political independence. As Africa becomes stronger politically and economically, its contribution to world culture will increase.

We have already suggested the remarkable harmony and
balance that traditional Africa achieved in the organization of
human relationships. By various means, Africans have succeeded in reducing tensions and resolving conflicts between
individuals and groups more effectively, it seems, than the
peoples of the West. The field of human relations is one of the
domains in which we believe, and hope, Africanity will make
valuable contributions to the common heritage of humanity. But
it certainly will not be the only one.

Bigomba, a Fulero man, playing *nzeze* (a kind of two-string zither). Itombwe region, Kivu province, Zaïre

Mwezi men threshing sorghum, Tanzania

Zulu women singing. Natal, Republic of South Africa

Obligatory labor during the colonial period. Women and men carrying bricks to the brick-kiln. Ndobogo, Rwanda

Nyamulinda, a diviner, uses knuckle-bones to predict what will happen to Semutwa. Uwisekuru, Rwanda

A diviner marks the forehead of his patient with kaolin, a propitious sign. Shwemu, Rwanda

Girls pounding manioc in a wooden mortar. Itombwe region, Kivu province, Zaïre

Weaver, Baule tribe, Ivory Coast

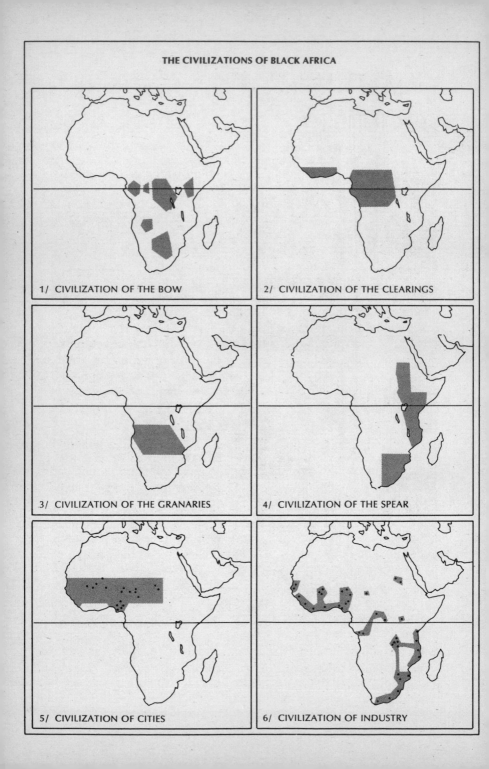

THE CIVILIZATIONS OF BLACK AFRICA

1/ CIVILIZATION OF THE BOW

2/ CIVILIZATION OF THE CLEARINGS

3/ CIVILIZATION OF THE GRANARIES

4/ CIVILIZATION OF THE SPEAR

5/ CIVILIZATION OF CITIES

6/ CIVILIZATION OF INDUSTRY

ONE HUNDRED TRADITIONAL SOCIETIES

Africanity interprets and synthesizes a complex of cultural phenomena. The Zulu warrior and the Fulani herdsman were not conscious of this, just as the peasant of Beauce and the craftsman of Tuscany were unaware that they were Europeans. But they were very much aware of their own societies, each of which had a name and territorial or psychological boundaries separating them from neighboring groups. These social and cultural realities are the material from which we construct the broader, more abstract concept of Africanity. In the process we must often turn back to the basic realities to be sure that we do not slip into the realm of imagination.

To enable the reader to share in this return to the basic realities, we present here a hundred societies of Black Africa, giving a very brief descriptive note for each. The number one hundred corresponds *very roughly* to about fifteen per cent of the total number of societies. But we do not claim that this sample is a representative statistical sample. The units have been selected not randomly but arbitrarily. Some of the larger units could have been divided so that they would be about the same size as the smaller ones. We did not do this because, not having sufficient information, we might very well have falsified the facts in making artificial divisions. And then, why should not traditional

Africa have had its France and its Luxembourg, its United States and its Guatemala, its China and its Laos?

The time described is the end of the traditional period, that is to say the decades immediately preceding 1885, the beginning of the colonial period for most of Black Africa. Even when the present tense is used, the traditional period is meant (except when otherwise indicated in the text).

Each entry has in parentheses, immediately after the name of the society, a term—bow, clearings, granaries, spear, cities—indicating the type of civilization to which the particular culture of the society belongs. This enables us to place each culture in one of the five large units into which, in our opinion, the several hundred actual societies of traditional Africa may be grouped. We have explained this point fully in an earlier work.* The reader can place the society on the appropriate map, by civilizations. The six maps are on page 140.

Reference to the civilization makes it unnecessary to repeat in each note the characteristics common to all the societies in that category. Thus our descriptions give the particular features of each society. Of course, the characteristics common to all the cultures in a civilization are manifested to a different degree in each of the cultures. In this order of abstraction from human phenomena, a certain degree of indefiniteness and approximation is inevitable; therefore one must bear in mind that a society is not placed in a specific civilization according to rigid criteria. Thus we should not be surprised to find in the civilization of cities the Dogon and the Bambara, who have never known urban settlements. As we have explained elsewhere, this civilization of the savannas of the Sudan manifests a basic duality. Two levels may be distinguished, each with a different orientation: on the first level, a limited economic system involving farming and herding and a political organization on the village scale; on a second level, the city-states oriented toward the outside world, acted as the terminals and crossroads of a communication network linking them with each other and with the Maghreb. Each of these levels is, more or less in each case,

* Maquet, *Civilizations of Black Africa*, op. cit.

economically independent of the other; in the areas near cities, rivers and trails, farming and urban activities are integrated by the ever-present influence of the city.*

There are also marginal cases: societies that because of certain features should be put into one civilization while because of others might just as well be put into another. In the text of the entries such ambiguities are pointed out where they occur.

Then follows a notation concerning the country or countries in which the heirs to each historical traditional culture are now residing. We have indicated in the text the extensions of the past into the present civilization of industry if they are especially prominent.

The uncertainty of our demographic information on African populations has often been stressed. We may add here that more recent estimates and censuses—those made during the process of decolonization and independence—are more reliable, but they have not always taken traditional affiliations into account. Thus our figures are often out of date and approximate. We give them when available only to convey some idea of the size of a society.

For the names of societies we have adopted the traditional English spelling when the names are known and used in English. When no spelling has become standardized, we have used a simplified phonetic spelling (letters from the Roman alphabet without any diacritic sign), and we have reduced words to their invariable radicals (thus *Luba*, not *Baluba; Kota*, not *Bakota*.) In this spelling *u* is pronounced as in "blue," *a* as in "father," *i* as in "machine," *e* as in "set," *s* always as in "sun," *g* always as in "good."

Jean-Claude Schalchli has drawn up the list of the hundred societies and prepared each entry. We are very grateful to him for his valuable help.

AGNI (clearings). Ivory Coast. 100,000. Like the Ashanti, the Baule and the Ewe, they are part of the Akan language group. They live in the Guinea forest and cultivate taro and bananas, which make up their basic diet. Their social organization is

* *Ibid.*, pp. 140 ff.

based on lineages living in scattered hamlets. Baked clay statuettes, probably of funerary significance, have been dug up in
Agni territory.

AMBA (clearings). Zaïre, Uganda. 60,000. The Amba live in the
forests of the western Rift Valley, not far from the Ruwenzori
Mountain Massif. Each individual takes his social and economic
status by reference to a patrilineage, whose members may be
scattered territorially in several villages. Exchange marriage
co-exists with marriage by bride wealth. The latter, favored by
Christian missionaries, seems to have been recently introduced
to the Amba.

AMBO (granaries). Zambia. 10,000. The Ambo are agriculturalists
in the fertile valleys of the Lukusashi, the Lunsemfwa and the
Luangwa. Cereals, the basis of their food economy, constitute
the only wealth of the six chiefdoms that share political power;
none of them has succeeded in gaining lasting supremacy over
its neighbors.

AMBO or OVAMBO (granaries). Angola. 175,000. Cultivators of
sorghum and millet, they also possess herds of cattle. Like their
neighbors to the north, the Mbundu, they belong both to the
civilization of the spear and the civilization of granaries. However they differ from the warrior herdsmen in this important
point: care of the cattle is not the work of men alone; women
share even in pastoral rituals.

ASHANTI (cities). Ghana. 800,000. This is a monarchical society
with Kumasi as the capital. The king and the princes became
famous in the past for the export of gold and slaves, sold to
European traffickers. Besides carved wooden dolls (akwa ba)
their art is the art of metal objects: weights for weighing gold
dust, copper and bronze urns, gold masks cast by the lost wax
process, hammered or repoussé pendants and other jewelry.
Oral literature is especially rich: Ashanti myths and tales are
among the most famous in West Africa.

BAGA (clearings). Guinea. 40,000. On the marshy low coast, from
the Rio Nunez to Conakry, the Baga grow rice, their basic food.
The rice fields are polders, reclaimed in the less humid areas.

Clearing is especially difficult: the marsh vegetation is cut down and burned, the roots are pulled up and dykes are built to cut off the rice field from the sea; then there is a waiting period of two or three years before the rice field is finally free of salt. The traditional Baga village is divided into "quarters" corresponding to the lineages governed by the elders. This structure is today too narrow to assimilate outside influences. Susu come from the interior and Fulani come down from the mountains to graze their salt-hungry flocks; the Muslims introduced their religion and the Catholics propagated theirs. Their art, as is the case throughout this part of Africa, is centered on carved masks connected with a secret initiation society, the simô.

BAMBARA (cities, peasant level). Guinea, Senegal, Mauritania, Upper Volta, Mali, Ivory Coast. One million. Spread over an area within a broad V bounded by the Lower Senegal and Niger, mainly clustered around Bamako, Ségou and Bougouni, the Bambara are millet farmers living in a complex symbiotic relationship with other peoples of the Western Sudan, especially the Fulani, both nomadic and sedentary, with whom they often intermarry. They played an important part in history, as was shown from the seventeenth century to the middle of the nineteenth by the formation of the Ségou and Kaarta empires, which were destroyed during the Tukulor invasions. Religion is very important in social life, as is evidenced by the many religious societies for initiation in several stages (dyo). Blacksmiths are also woodworkers. Art is strongly religious in character. One of the most widespread motifs in sculpture is the stylized antelope. Angular geometric forms are very common in Bambara sculpture and other arts.

BAMILEKE (cities, peasant level). Cameroon. 450,000. Practicing agriculture and the raising of sheep and goats, the Bamileke live on the western plateaus of Cameroon at an altitude of 3600 to 4500 feet. The population density is very high (121 per square mile), and rapid demographic expansion has promoted large-scale emigration to industrial centers. These people are organized in chiefdoms, of which the oldest, such as Bafoussam, traditionally play the most important role. But in the seventeenth century their rivalry prevented them from effectively resisting the invasion of the Bamum, conquering warriors who were better organized politically: some peoples had to submit, while others fled to the hills. At present their rate of population increase presents social and political problems to the national government at Yaoundé, against which they form a constantly resurgent opposition. Statues of chiefs, large carved drums, stools, masks and granary doors are well known to art lovers, as are ivory horns, bracelets and statuettes.

BAMUM (cities). Cameroon. 85,000. Now living in the west in the region of Foumban, their capital, these aggressive warriors about three centuries ago conquered a number of Bamileke chiefdoms, thanks to their more centralized political and military organization. They founded a kingdom and, the king, assisted by ministers and supported by a military aristocracy, was able to create a truly centralized state. The most famous monarch, the Sultan Njoya, was converted to Islam. He is most famous for having invented an original writing system based on a thirty-letter alphabet, which he used for his administration. On his orders, scribes wrote a history and description of the kingdom. Dance masks, worn on top of the head, are of carved wood or baked clay, or even cast in bronze by the lost wax process. Among them are found smiling masks, probably the only ones in Africa. The decorative motifs are often stylized animals. Boxes, doors and stools are intricately carved.

BAULE (clearings). Ivory Coast. 400,000. Forest and savanna cultivators, related to the Ashanti and the Agni, the Baule live in the Bouaké region. Matrilineal descent predominates. Aesthetic values permeate everyday life, being expressed in objects of utility and personal adornment. Baule art is varied: graceful female statuettes, wooden urns carved in relief, black masks in polished wood, red- and white-painted masks, stools, doors. Brass figurines used to weigh gold dust are comparable to those made by the Ashanti.

BEMBA (granaries). Zambia. 150,000. The Bemba's political system may be described as a federation of chiefdoms, each one forming a state with a permanent coercive organization supported by tribute from conquered villages. The paramount chief of the federation has mainly judicial powers; he also acts as arbiter in conflicts between chiefdoms; his preeminence is based on descent that is traced matrilineally back to an ancestress. To clear the forest they use an elaborate system of burning, the *chitimene*.

BINGA (bow). Cameroon, Zaïre, Congo, Gabon. 27,000. These Pygmy hunters and gatherers live scattered in the equatorial forest from the Atlantic coast to a line from the Congo to the Ubangi. Grouped in small bands, they have no political organization. They neither farm nor raise stock. Their only domestic animal is the dog, used for hunting. Some groups maintain a close relationship with the neighboring agricultural populations; in Cameroon, for example, they exchange meat of wild animals for bananas or other food. When these trading relationships become permanent, a true clientship is established, and the Binga then tend to settle on the outskirts of villages.

BINI (cities). Nigeria. 400,000. Living in the fertile area of the Gulf of Guinea, the Bini are especially noted for their part in building the celebrated Benin Empire around the twelfth century; their traditions may be directly traced to it. The *Oba*, who still rule today, are the heirs of a dynasty that goes back to Ife. Discovered only in 1897, Benin art is today appreciated throughout the world. Its most characteristic forms are ivory masks, commemorative bronze heads supporting carved tusks and plaques, also in bronze, representing kingly or military themes. It was from Ife that Benin learned, about 1280, the technique of lost wax casting. The bronzes were cast by craftsmen organized professionally under hereditary chiefs. The making of plaques was a ritual included in the *oba's* enthronement ceremonies; they were made to decorate the deceased *oba's* altar.

BIRA (clearings). Zaïre. 45,000. The Bira of the plains, who settled in the Shari plain west of Lake Albert, are distinguished from the Bira of the forest, who live west of them between the Lenda and the Epulu rivers. The former are cultivators, but their frequent contacts with Hima pastoralists enabled them to take up herding. The forest Bira live by agriculture only; thanks to the ivory which they obtain from Pygmy hunters, with whom they trade, they lead a generally easy life. Politically, neither group recognizes any authority higher than the head of the lineage, assisted by the elders.

BOBO (cities, peasant level). Mali, Upper Volta. 45,000. The Bobo cultivate millet and fonio and also gather. Their society, with no political organization beyond that of the village governed by the elders, offered little resistance to the assault of the Sudanese empires. For a long time they were victims of the slave trade. Their sculpture is mainly represented by large wooden masks, related in style to those of the Dogon. Usually painted red, white and black, some represent animals, while others are decorated only with geometrical motifs of heraldic significance.

BUSHMEN (bow). South Africa, Southwest Africa, Mozambique. 10,000. Hunters and gatherers, who a few centuries ago occupied the whole end of the continent south of the Zambezi, the Bushmen were driven back, first by agricultural peoples (especially the Tswana) and then by the Europeans, who are gradually exterminating them. The survivors are now slaves of the Tswana, except for a few—10,000 at the most—who still carry on their traditional way of life in the Kalahari Desert, the Drakensberg and the desert areas of Southwest Africa. The best known are the Naron and the Namib. Their social unit is the hunting band led by a chief chosen for his skill or his influence. At one time the groups were united in a sort of federation directed by the council of elders that settled differences between groups, decided on important migrations and exercised a sort of ultimate social control. Today each group lives independently of the others. The pursuit of game, which is now extremely scarce, and the search for water sources determine movements.

CHOKWE (granaries). Angola, Zaïre. 600,000. In the nineteenth century the Chokwe founded a centralized, monarchical state in the savannas between the Kouilou and the Kasai. Its wealth depended on tributary peoples. They were in almost constant competition with the kingdom of their neighbors, the Lunda, who still dispute their hegemony in this area. Villages are important in the Chokwe kingdom. The people produce remarkable masks and very unusual carved chairs.

CHWEZI (spear). Uganda. These people, now extinct, founded the kingdom of Kitara, ancestral to Nyoro. They are known to historians only because of traditions of the Great Lakes kingdoms and to archeologists because of excavations at Bigo and Masaka in Uganda. The kingdom of Kitara seems to have covered the whole area between Lakes Edward, Albert, Kyoga and Victoria, north of the equator, and perhaps even part of Nkole. Excavations have revealed a society expert in the art of terracing (ditches, fortifications) and stonework (wells cut through rock). Traditions recall a stratified structure comprising at least one ruling class of pastoralists and a lower class of agricultural serfs. The king's person was sacred, and administration was centralized. These features are still found in the kingdoms in this area. The kingdom of Kitara and its Chwezi rulers disappeared at the time of the Luo invasions in the late fifteenth and the early sixteenth centuries.

DAN (clearings). Liberia, Ivory Coast. 200,000. The Dan live on an isolated, rain-forested plain dominated in the Man region by a mountain mass with peaks over 3000 feet high. They clear the forest and cultivate rice, and since the beginning of this century they have adopted some commercial crops, coffee and cotton. Each village contains only one lineage, the chief of which, when he is powerful, extends his authority over several related villages. Dan masks, carved in wood, are often connected with the *poro* institution, as with the Mende, and play an important part in religious life and in social control. The best known are ancestor masks, but some have a special function, such as the thunder mask.

DINKA (spear). Sudan. 500,000. Pastoralists, fishermen and agriculturalists, the Dinka, who are neighbors of the Nuer, live in the marshy regions of the White Nile and the Bahr-el-Ghazal. Extreme poverty of material culture accompanies a great wealth

of mythology and religious poetry. There is no political authority at the head of this collection of groups, which, however,
constitute a cultural, linguistic and religious unit. In each group
two social classes may be distinguished: the priests, the guard-
ians of the ritual of the sacred harpoon, and the warriors, the
commoners.

DOGON (cities, peasant level). Mali. 200,000. Living in the cliffs
of Bandiagara in the Mopti region, these Sudan agriculturalists
are famous for their great religious masks surmounted by a sort
of Cross of Lorraine. Worn at funerals, these masks are closely
linked with an extremely rich agrarian mythology. The village
and the extended family are the basis of the social organization.
The *hogon*, who is both priest and chief, performs the highest
religious and judicial functions. The blacksmiths, who are
looked at with both scorn and awe, form a separate group.
Woodworking as well as iron-working is their special skill;
they do not till the land. The Dogon possess a lore, esoteric and
very elaborate, on the origins of man and the world. Their
strong interest in the aesthetic is manifested in beautiful carved
wooden doorlocks, doors decorated with human or animal motifs and certain statues, especially those of the Tellem, ancestors
of the Dogon.

EKOI (clearings). Cameroon, Nigeria. 100,000. Forest cultivators
on the banks of the Upper Cross River, the Ekoi have a social
organization based on lineage. As in many societies in this area,
social control is effected through so-called secret societies, which
also perform the initiation ceremonies for young people. One
of these organizations, the *Egbo*, is widespread throughout
southern Nigeria and is believed to be of Ekoi origin. Symbolized
by masks, which are brought out at harvest time and for initiation ceremonies, it is also a focus of religious life.

EWE (cities, peasant level). Togo, Dahomey, Ghana. 800,000.
The Ewe live in a region of broad, open spaces suitable for
cultivating palm trees, on the coast of the Benin Gulf between
the two large forest zones of Equatorial Africa and Guinea. This
is the home of the great kingdoms of Benin, Ife and Dahomey.

The Ewe did not remain outside these major political groupings but constituted the subjugated lower caste. Their chiefdoms, though influenced by the principles of aristocracy and monarchy, formed a federation governed by a great council of chiefs.

FALI (cities, peasant level). Cameroon. 36,000. Living at the southern end of the mountain massifs of Adamawa, the Fali are part of the heterogeneous people usually called the *Kirdi* (pagans, meaning non-Muslim). They are rice farmers. Driven back by Muslim invaders into the impregnable mountains, the Fali live in villages clinging to the rocky cliffs of the mountains. The kinship structure, patrilineal and patrilocal, is reflected by the landscape; a hamlet corresponds to each lineage. The house, surrounded by a dry stone wall enclosing granaries, kitchens and dwelling rooms of baked clay symbolizes in its layout this society's view of the world. Their art is best represented by their music. Pottery is made by women, who do not specialize in the craft.

FANG (clearings). Gabon, Cameroon. 160,000. One of the best-known peoples of the group called Pahouin (Pangwe, Fang, Beti, Bulu), which comprises over 800,000 individuals divided between Cameroon, Gabon, Congo and Equatorial Guinea, the Fang live in the great rain forest, which they clear by burning. They practice slash-and-burn agriculture with long fallowing. By a careful spacing of crops throughout the year, the agricultural cycle provides them with a regular food supply. Recently coconut plantations have been successfully established. Sculpture consists of masks and ancestor statues. Drums and stools are carved in semi-relief.

FON (cities). Dahomey, Togo. 900,000. The Fon built up the kingdom of Dahomey, a monarchical society with a complex and authoritarian organization, set up in the seventeenth century, did not collapse until the period of European colonization. From his capital, Abomey, the king reigned absolutely through seven high officials paralleled by seven women, whom protocol placed before the men in ceremonies. Provinces, regions and villages were administered by hierarchical chiefs, all dependent on the king. A large, specialized pantheon corresponded in the religious sphere to this highly developed political centralization. Art exalted the kings and their exploits: low-reliefs of the palace of Abomey in unfired clay, large statues of kings and gods.

FULANI or FOULBE or PEUL (cities). Senegal, Mali, Guinea, Upper Volta, Dahomey, Niger, Nigeria, Cameroon. The racial origin of the Fulani is in dispute. As nomadic pastoralists they spread through the Western Sudan, from Senegal to Chad, from the thirteenth century on. Their migrations brought them into contact with many populations, with whom they intermarried. Today they are nearly all sedentary, except for a few groups such as the Bororo Fulani of Adamawa, and have often become agriculturalists. In the past the Fulani founded great nations, such as the kingdoms of Macina, Futa-Djalon, Futa-Toro or Adamawa. Their language is understood by nearly all the peoples of Western and Central Sudan and thus allows communication throughout that vast area. The Fulani also played an important role in the diffusion of Islam.

GALLA (spear). Ethiopia. Three million. Traditionally pastoralists and warriors, the Galla invaded the Ethiopian plateau about the sixteenth century. They posed a grave threat to the Christian kingdom of Abyssinia, but were finally subjugated at the end of the nineteenth century. Even today the central government has trouble exercising authority over some not easily accessible Galla areas. The Galla have integrated only slightly with the Christian or Muslim population. In the old Galla society, a king, the *Abba Bokou*, who held office for only eight years, proclaimed the law, dispensed justice and commanded the army in time of war. A preoccupation with war dominated the education of the young men, who were organized in age classes and went through successive periods of initiation. Some Galla groups have become sedentary and taken to agriculture.

GANDA (spear). Uganda. One million. Founded by a group of Luo warrior herdsmen about the beginning of the sixteenth century, the Ganda kingdom has grown considerably over three centuries. Its king, the *Kabaka*, controls all political power. Unlike its neighbors, Ganda society has become homogeneous: it is not divided into hierarchical strata. Its wealth and cohesion enabled it to preserve its special character and its supremacy in the present state of Uganda, which, except for the kingdom of Buganda, was formed by other traditional monarchies, notably those of the Nyoro, the Toro and the Nkole. Mutesa II, the King of Buganda, was also president of the federal state of Uganda until the coup of 1966. He died in exile in London in 1969.

GIKUYU (spear). Kenya. One million. The Gikuyu culture, essentially based on cattle, is typical of the East African "cattle complex" often described by anthropologists. Wars against neighboring groups—the Masai in this case—took the form of raids to seize cattle or to obtain the use of good pasture land. Though not much blood was shed, these raids were extremely frequent and determined the population patterns of the region. The internal social life of these groups was also influenced by pastoral and military values. Thus the original system of government by age classes so well described by Jomo Kenyatta, now president of Kenya, had first and foremost a military function. Although Gikuyu society has never produced a truly centralized political authority, its cohesion enabled it to play a determining role in the recent political development of Kenya.

GURO (clearings). Ivory Coast. 115,000. West of the Baule country, straddling the forest areas of the south and the Sudan highlands of the north, live the agriculturalist Guro. Each village is politically autonomous, but alliances and kinship have worked in such a way that certain chiefs have gained a predominating influence. Culturally they are related to the Baule. Their polychrome or polished wood masks are characterized by rounded foreheads and curvilinear features.

HAUSA (cities) Nigeria, Niger. 600,000. Colonies of Hausa traders are now established all over Western and Central Sudan. They were farmers and built fortified towns in which crafts played an important economic role. The most famous of these towns, which lie between the River Niger and Lake Chad, are Kano, Zaria and Katsena. The kings who ruled these towns converted

to Islam and from the eleventh to the nineteenth century resisted attempted invasions by other Sudanese peoples, especially
the Songhai in the sixteenth century.

HAYA (spear). Tanzania. 300,000. Originally this term was applied only to the fishermen of the southwest shore of Lake
Victoria, but now the name designates the inhabitants of several
small kingdoms (Karagwe, Kiziba, Ihangiro, etc.) comprising
three strata: the dynastic, pastoral and agricultural clans. In
1889 an epidemic destroyed nearly all the livestock, so the Haya
country became almost exclusively agricultural. For over a century robusta coffee has been cultivated; the kings have a monop-
oly on its export and thus obtain all the profits.

HERERO (spear). Southwest Africa. 30,000 (estimated, 1967).
During the war waged against the Herero by the Germans, from
1904 to 1906, their numbers decreased from 100,000 to 25,000.
The Herero are nomadic pastoralists, and all their activities are
directed to the care of livestock and the search for pasture.
Unlike most East African pastoralists, they did not form an
aristocratic kingdom based on conquest by war. Their way of
life resembles that of some of the Nilotic peoples, such as the
Nuer: a cult of the sacred fire of the ancestors, guarded day and
night by women. They recognize double descent, patrilineal and
matrilineal. Their leather garments are decorated with amazingly
heavy metal ornaments and pendants.

HIMA (spear). Rwanda, Uganda. These pastoralists invaded the
Great Lakes area before the Luo and apparently are related to
the Chwezi. In the nineteenth century some Hima groups still
led a nomadic life, especially in the Lake Albert area and Northeast Rwanda. Other Hima groups had been integrated into the
social stratification of certain kingdoms in the same area, where
they constituted the governing class (in the Nyoro, Nkole and
Zinza societies) or the group immediately below the rulers (in
the Toro society). In a few cases they played a subordinate role,
tending other people's cattle, as in the Soga states.

HOTTENTOT (spear). South Africa, Southwest Africa. 20,000. This
name describes a number of pastoral peoples who once occupied

the whole western part of Southern Africa. After driving back the Bushmen into the desert areas, they are now themselves on the way to extinction. Four main groups are distinguishable by linguistic criteria: the Nama, the Korana, the Gona and the Cape Hottentot, the last now extinct. They are nomadic, constantly in search of pasture. They corral their cattle in camps surrounded by a circular fence of thorny bushes. They do not raise cattle for meat; the milk is drunk clotted; berries and roots complete their diet. Unlike the East African pastoralists, where the care of cattle is strictly the province of men, the women do the milking among the Hottentots. The Hottentots speak a click language, resembling that of the Bushmen, and in their physical type they belong to the Khoisan race.

IBIBIO (clearings). Nigeria. Over 1 million. Living in the forest belt east of the River Niger, the Ibibio are agriculturalists and tree planters; they are also well known as accomplished traders. They have many characteristics in common with their neighbors, the Ibo. Men's clubs such as the *Ekpo* hold political power; their strength is symbolized by masks, dance headdresses and statues. Some statues have articulated jaws and limbs. The masks are brought out at funerals of chiefs, and are used to punish violations of social rules, such as theft or adultery.

IBO (clearings). Nigeria. 5,500,000. Settled in the forest belt of the Niger delta, the Ibo mostly cultivate various species of yams. The main social unit is the territorially based patrilineage. The *Mmo* society comprises a group of men who put on masks and impersonate the ancestors. Besides being an initiation society, this organization is also, as almost everywhere in West Africa, an agent of social control, concerned especially with the suppression of witchcraft.

IJO or IJAW (clearings). Nigeria. 300,000. The Ijo were apparently driven back into their present habitat by Yoruba invaders. They constitute a warlike society in which secret societies play an essential part, organizing important ceremonies on the death of a chief, at the defeat of an enemy or after a successful elephant hunt. The most solemn rituals celebrate water spirits: they occur regularly within a cycle of twenty-five years. Still practiced today, these celebrations include dances—some of them performed in the water—in which highly stylized masks, cubist in form, are used. The same bold style is found in altars devoted to ancestor worship: they are built of cylinders and cubes put together in a frame.

KISI (clearings). Guinea, Sierra Leone, Liberia. 200,000. Living on the borders of the Atlantic forest and the Sudan savanna, the Kisi "the rice people" practice slash-and-burn agriculture with rotation of crops and several years' fallowing. Kinship is the basis of social and political life. Ancestor worship and agrarian rituals merge on the lineage level; the lineage is also an economic unit. In their religious activities the Kisi use stone statuettes called *pomdo*, like those found in Mende country. The origin of these "Kisi stones" is not yet known.

KONGO (granaries). Congo, Zaïre, Angola. Three million. Grain farmers, the Kongo had built up a large kingdom at the mouth of the Congo long before the fifteenth century: it had already reached its apogee when the Portuguese landed in the area in 1482. The capital Mbanza Kongo then dominated six provinces between the ocean, the River Congo, the Bengo and the Kwango. The economy of the kingdom was based on agricultural produce, but trade and craftsmanship were also important. The circulation of cowrie shells and raffia cloth formed a sort of monetary system. Despite the excellent relationship between the Kongo kingdom and the early Portuguese settlers, a troubled period resulted in the decay of this remarkable political organization from the sixteenth to the nineteenth century. Today the Kongo still play an important political role. Akabo, the party of the late President Kasavubu of the Democratic Republic of Congo (now Zaïre), which was one of the most active political organizations at the end of the Belgian colonization, is the main political organ of Kongo society. In Congo-Brazzaville it is enough to recall the name of former President Fulbert Youlou to indicate the important political role of the Kongo.

KOTA (clearings). Gabon, Congo, 38,000. This name is applied not so much to one society as to a number of related groups speaking languages of the same family. The Kota live in a forest area east of the Fang, who were stronger than they, and from whom they borrowed many culture traits. Their sculpture, unlike Fang sculpture, is decorative and abstract: the parts of the human body are merely suggested by geometrical forms. Their secret societies have today lost their significance, and the many masks still circulating in Kota territory are now used only for entertainment.

KOTOKO (cities). Chad, Cameroon, Nigeria. 25,000. The term Kotoko, of Arabic origin, designates a collection of groups that number the Sao among their ancestors. City-dwellers and fishermen, they are settled along the banks of the Logone and the Chari. The Sao are credited with the invention of walled cities: a Sao is said to have built the wall around Kano, a Hausa city. At Goulfeil the wall is still kept in repair: it is amazingly massive in a land without stone where timber is scarce. Recent excavations have revealed a rich body of Sao art: expressive statuettes of baked clay, animal figures and bronze ornaments.

KPELLE (in Guinea called by the French form of the name, Guerzé) (clearings). Liberia, Guinea. 100,000. These agriculturalists are related to the Dan, Mende and Kisi peoples; they have in common the *Poro* institution, a secret initiation society. Like that of their neighbors, their sculpture consists mainly of masks, which are brought out of the forests for initiation ceremonies.

KUBA (granaries). Zaïre. 75,000. The Kuba are a group of peoples sometimes called by ethnographers Bushong or Mbala, these being the most important groups. The Kuba chiefdoms recognize the supremacy of the chief of the Mbala, the *Nyimi*, and pay tribute to him. A group of nobles alone have access to government office. Kuba art reflects this social organization: sculptors make luxury objects (cups in the form of heads, cosmetic boxes) for the nobility and works symbolizing the glory of chiefs (statues of kings, scepters).

LOBI (cities, peasant level). Upper Volta, Ivory Coast, Ghana. 150,000. On the poor, lateritic soils of the Sudan belt, the Lobi grow fonio, "the most wretched of cereals." They regularly supplement their diet by hunting and gathering. In this region of great political powers, their poverty has kept them from the great historical ventures, in which, like their neighbors the Bobo and the Coniagui, they played only a passive role, supplying tribute and slaves to the more highly organized invaders. Their culture is that typical of the peasants of the civilization of cities. Their art consists of wood sculpture, especially three-legged stools decorated with a head wearing the helmet-shaped head-dress common in this area.

LOZI (granaries). Zambia. 180,000. In the Zambezi valley, one chiefdom stronger than its neighbors became a kingdom that dominated others, in particular the Rotse. The king has extensive powers, and a government of local officials rules various regions in his name. The dignitaries are arranged in a meticulous hier-archy. The government's essential role is to drain off the eco-nomic surplus to the capital, where it is used to keep up the government machinery.

LUBA (granaries). Zaïre, Zambia. Three million. The Luba founded one of the historical empires of the savannas south of the equatorial forest. Their rich, refined art expresses the values of kinship. At the end of the nineteenth century the Chokwe invasion put an end to their hegemony. Luba traditions, how-ever, have remained strong enough to enable them to oppose the Lunda, who were used by the Katanga secessionists, since 1960.

LULUA (granaries). Zaïre. 500,000. The Lulua, for a long time tributaries of the Kuba kingdoms, are organized on the village level. Certain important chiefdoms ensure social cohesion. Their finely carved ancestor figures are perhaps the best African ex-amples of harmony between form and decoration. The style of their masks seems to have been borrowed from the Kuba.

LUNDA (granaries). Angola, Zaïre, Zambia. 700,000. These savan-na agriculturalists, borrowed the institution of kingship from their neighbors, the Luba, and founded, in the seventeenth cen-tury, a great empire extending from the Kwango to Lake Moëro.

Their art, consisting mostly of prestige and luxury objects, is represented by wood sculpture. The late Moïse Tshombe, who was related to the ruling lineage of the Lunda, appealed to tribal loyalty to win the support of the Lunda in his attempted secession of Katanga.

LUO (spear). Kenya, Tanzania. 800,000. Settled on the eastern shore of Lake Victoria around the Gulf of Kavirondo, the Luo played an important historical role in the whole area between Bahr-el-Ghazal and Lake Victoria. Originally from the Rumbeck area in the south of the Sudanese Republic, by the sixteenth century their long migrations had brought them to the Great Lakes area, which they entered from the north, between Lakes Albert and Kyoga. Overthrowing the Kitara and driving out the Chwezi, they founded the Nyoro kingdom ruled by the Bito dynasty. From this center the Bito spread out and formed several peripheral kingdoms, one of which was to become Buganda. The population now called Luo is not organized into a kingdom.

MALINKE (cities). Senegal, Mali, Guinea, Portuguese Guinea, Ivory Coast. One million. Also called Mandingo or Mande, the Malinke founded the famous Keita dynasty that reigned over the Mali empire; their hegemony over Western Sudan followed that of Ghana. Important cities, such as Mali, the capital, Timbuktu and Djenne, lived by trading; they were also flourishing intellectual centers. Ancient Mali, weakened in the fifteenth century by pressure from the Tuareg, the Mossi and the Songhai, left epic traditions on which the political leaders of modern Mali, such as the former President Modibu Keita, prided themselves. The Mali empire is still an example for supporters of the idea of a great West African political complex.

MANGBETU (clearings and spear). Zaïre. The Mangbetu are settled in the Ituri forest where they grow root crops and raise sheep and goats. Coming from the north like their neighbors, the Zande, they claim to be descendants of the mythical founder of a monarchy. Their society comprised an aristocratic ruling class, to whom the commoners paid tribute. In the nineteenth century they were unable to resist a Zande invasion. Now they have a symbiotic relationship with Mbuti hunters, certain groups of whom have become their clients: they exchange hand-crafted objects with the Mbuti for the meat of wild animals.

MASAI (spear). Kenya, Tanzania. 180,000. The Masai are cattle herders. They have built up a social and political organization based on a highly developed age-class system. All the boys circumcised at a certain time belong to the same class, which covers a period of about seven years. They can marry only after their class has fulfilled its military duties for two periods of seven years, by which time they are about thirty years old. As with other pastoralists in the civilization of the spear, cattle have a high social value, but they also play an important economic role: milk, butter, cheese and blood constitute the regular diet. The Masai often fought against their neighbors the Gikuyu.

MBUNDU (granaries). Angola. 1,300,000. The Mbundu are agri-culturalists and pastoralists. They resemble the savanna societies in that they cultivate cereals and hold important the villages, which are often the seats of large chiefdoms; they share the pastoral peoples' high regard for cattle. Cattle hold a privileged economic position; they are used to pay bride wealth and are indispensable for social prestige.

MBUTI or EFE (bow). Zaïre. 32,000. The Mbuti, a Pygmy people, live in the Ituri forest, and even those groups in continuous contact with agriculturalists do not cultivate the land. The men hunt with bow and arrow, individually or in small groups. Sometimes they set traps and organize beats for large game. The women are usually responsible for gathering fruits, roots and wild tubers. The social unit is based on the hunting group and their close relatives. Camps are not fixed, and no exact territory belongs to any one group; the groups move to new hunting grounds as required. Within the group, there is no chief holding power; authority is quite diffuse. The groups are related to each other by marriage ties, and marriage is usually by exchange of women. As with all hunters, their way of life is doomed to extinction.

MENDE (clearings). Sierra Leone, Liberia. 580,000. The Mende grow rice in the rain forest, and rice cultivation fills the year and sets the seasons. There is no centralized government: the group is united only by a common language and culture. An important feature of their culture is the *Poro*, an initiation society with a very important social function: the socialization of the young (religious and agricultural training) and the preservation of customs and social harmony. Mende art is especially famous for imaginatively decorated head masks worn by women at girls' initiation ceremonies.

MONGO (clearings). Zaïre. 1,500,000. In the forest region between the Congo, the Kasai and the Lualaba rivers, the Mongo lead the life of forest cultivators. The Mongo people is actually made up of several groups, such as the Hamba or Tetela. Although there is no central political authority to maintain the unity of the many groups scattered throughout the clearings, there is real unity among the Mongo. It is confirmed by the kinship system: all call themselves descendants of the same ancestor Mongo. Their history is a long list of genealogies, confused by distance and competition for seniority, but it still supports a very strong social cohesion.

MOSSI (cities). Upper Volta. 1,700,000. Traditionally, the Mossi formed two states of which the capitals Ouagadougou and Ouahigouya were ruled by a chief with both religious and political functions. He reigned over a population of peasants subjugated by a powerful aristocratic chivalry. Today they are still dominant in Upper Volta—President Yameogo is of Mossi origin —and their culture enjoys a privileged situation unusual in sub-Saharan Africa: in their territory traditionalism and nationalism smoothly converge. In the past, the Mossi peacefully resisted Malinke and Songhai invasions and assimilated their institutions. Craftsmanship is still very much alive in the hands of specialists who form closed groups: blacksmiths, whose wives are potters, jewelers, carpenters, basket-weavers, dyers. The nobles supply the nucleus of a vigorous administration. The farmers grow mainly millet, sorghum and groundnuts.

NANDI (spear). Kenya, Tanzania. 115,000. Neighbors of the Masai, east of Lake Victoria, they have borrowed many features of Masai culture, especially the military age-class system and cattle rituals. They also cultivate rice. They have often been victims of Masai invasions.

NGALA (clearings). Zaïre. 110,000. Ngala villages are scattered throughout the area between the Congo and the Ubangi in the equatorial forest. Each individual has his place in a complex network of kinship relations that exactly define his rights and duties with regard to each person. Marriages create relations of reciprocity between the various lineages; these relationships persist through the generations.

NGONI (granaries). Tanzania, Zambia, Malawi. 200,000. The name designates the descendants of Zulu groups who fled the rule of Chief Chaka at the end of the nineteenth century. Today the Ngoni are as much agriculturalists as they are herders of sheep, goats and cattle. Their traditions connect them with the pastoral peoples of East Africa, in that social prestige is bound up with cattle ownership. Because of the importance they attach to agriculture, they are classed in the civilization of granaries.

NGU (spear). Tanzania. Close neighbors of the Masai, the Ngu are warrior herdsmen who are not organized as a monarchy. They place great stress on age classes. Initiation, which marks the beginning of a new class, is of capital importance. The instructors impress their teachings on the memory of their pupils by teaching them very short songs which they illustrate with expressive clay figurines.

NKOLE (spear). Uganda. 260,000. In the mountainous region between Lakes Edward and Victoria, Nkole pastoralists have built up an aristocratic, monarchical political structure. Stratification in closed castes is more marked than in other states in the area. For example, mariage is forbidden between the Hima pastoralists and the Iru agriculturalists; only the Iru pay taxes; the profession of arms is reserved for the Hima; in social relationships there is strict segregation. Within the upper caste there is a feudal relationship between the king and the Hima pastoralists. This takes the form of personal ties of protection and assistance and consolidates the unity of the ruling caste. The king preserves harmony among his dependants and protects them against outsiders; in return he receives their homage, their military assistance and sometimes gifts of cattle.

NOK (cities). Nigeria. This term designates not a society but a village in Nigeria south of the central plateau, 95 miles southwest of the Jos mines. In 1943 a great number of baked clay statues came to light in the subsoil of the village. According to carbon 14 dating, these statues date back to a period from 900 B.C. to A.D. 200. The culture to which they belong is named after the village. Like the Ife heads, the Nok statues are life size. These are the only known cases in Africa of ceramic statuary of such dimensions. Other stylistic similarities have led archeologists to conclude that the Nok and Ife cultures are probably two collateral branches descended from an older civilization.

NUER (spear). Sudan. 300,000. Though their economic system is based as much on agriculture as on pastoralism, the Nuer regard cattle as the supreme form of wealth: only men are allowed to tend them, and they are the basis for all social values. Cattle products (milk and blood, sometime mixed) are consumed, but meat is eaten only on special occasions. The importance of cattle is reflected in their vocabulary: twenty-seven terms are not enough for these pastoralists to designate the various possible markings on the animals' coats. The material culture of this Nilotic people, who live in the marshy plains of the Upper Nile, is very poor. They go naked. There is no political authority to hold power: the homogeneity of each group is maintained by the necessity of defending their herds together.

NYORO (spear). Uganda. 110,000. The Nyoro kingdom, which succeeded the Kitara, was set up by Luo invaders. The Bito are the reigning dynasty. In Bunyoro we find a divine monarchy surrounded by a court, but without a fixed capital, and stratification into two castes; the pastoralists, who are descended from the conquerors, form the upper caste. The Bunyoro kingdom predated the Buganda, which split off from it; in the nineteenth century Buganda wrested from Bunyoro its supremacy in the region.

NZIMA (clearings). Ghana, Ivory Coast. 12,000. This society of forest cultivators lives around the mouth of the River Tano.

Like its neighbors, the Ashanti, Agni and Baule, it belongs to the Akan group. Kwame Nkruma was of Nzima origin.

PENDE (clearings). Zaïre. 27,000. In the savannas of the upper Kwilu, Pende cultivators are organized in hereditary chiefdoms. They are famous for their wood sculpture. They make two kinds of masks: "real" masks worn by dancers and decorated with a thick raffia headdress and miniature masks of ivory, or even cast in copper, lead or brass; the latter are amulets, worn around the neck.

REGA (clearings). Zaïre. The Rega live in the forest belt northeast of Lake Tanganyika. Although, as with all forest peoples, the basic social units are the village and the lineage, some chiefs have gained supremacy. They are respected judges rather than true political chiefs; nevertheless, their activities favor a sort of federal organization.

RUNDI (spear). Burundi. Two million. Rundi society was divided into four strata: the princes (abaganwa), the nobles (tutsi), the peasants and artisans (hutu) and the hunters and potters (twa). A monarchical organization was set up at a late stage, in the nineteenth century; with the feudal institution of the ubugabire it succeeded in creating a very stable social structure that survived through the decolonization period: until the military coup d'état of 1966 the new Rundi state was a kingdom the king of which, Mwambutsa, reigned from 1915 to 1966. The Burundi, whose traditional structures and colonial history are very similar to those of their northern neighbors, the Rwanda, split off from Rwanda after independence.

RWANDA (spear) Rwanda. Two million. In the mountainous area of the Congo-Nile watershed east of Lake Kivu, Tutsi warrior herdsmen around the sixteenth century built up a three-caste state of the same type as the neighboring kingdom of Nkole. Under the royal dynasty of the Nyiginya, the Tutsi formed a warrior nobility who did not cultivate the land but appropriated the agricultural surplus of the Hutu peasants (about 85% of the population) through the feudal institution called ubuhake: a pastoralist gave protection to a peasant by granting him possession of a cow, while reserving ownership for himself; in return, the peasant became his dependant, paying him regular tribute in agricultural products and labor. This constituted severe exploitation and was resented by the Hutu. Thus, in spite of the support given by the Belgian colonial administration to the Tutsi, who held political office, a peasant revolt broke out in November 1959, before independence, and, due to the electoral victory of the Hutu party (Parmehutu), a republic was proclaimed; the Tutsi minorities were stripped of their political powers and in some cases persecuted and driven out. This change of regime, helped in the later stages by outside pressures, gave rise to violent feelings that have not yet been allayed.

SARAKOLE or SONINKE (cities). Mali. 360,000. The Sarakole are a branch of the large Mende group. Their origin is difficult to place exactly; they may result from interbreeding with Berbers. They founded the Ghana Empire, which dominated the sub-Saharan steppes for a large part of the European Middle Ages. The empire was mentioned in a ninth-century Arab text that calls it the land of gold; it broke up in the thirteenth century after the destruction of its capital, located on the site of Kumbi (about 217 miles north of modern Bamako) by Sundiata, the Malinke king of Mali. Ghana's wealth in gold was responsible for the constant stream of caravans that crossed the Sahara to profitably exchange goods with North Africa: gold, ivory and slaves for salt, cloth, copper, dates and figs. The king held considerable power, for his wealth enabled him to maintain a large army and to employ skilled craftsmen to make effective weapons. In the nineteenth century the Sarakole formed a centralized state through the initiative of a brilliant military chief, Samory, who was born about 1830. The countries he conquered, divided into districts and provinces, were ruled by his administrators. The army was organized into regiments and detachments. With it he was able to extend his power to the left bank of the Niger, where he ran into French columns occupying the river valley. Driven into Upper Guinea and the north of the Ivory Coast, he was finally captured at Guélémou in 1898. In his last years, hunted down by the French, he was regarded as a bandit chief.

SENUFO (cities, peasant level). Ivory Coast, Mali, Upper Volta. 350,000. The Senufo are agriculturalists in the Sudan savanna; their chief crops are rice in the south and millet in the north. They form part of the peasant masses who provided one of the economic bases of the great empires of West Africa. Senufo culture has retained its own singular quality, preserved by skilled craftsman who are organized into groups specializing in wood or copper work. Their masks are often used for initiation; they are ornately carved and usually painted in black on a red background. One of the commonest motifs is a hornbill, often seen on wooden boxes in which women keep *karite* butter and on heddle pulleys for looms.

SERER (cities, peasant level). Senegal. 265,000. The Serer cultivate the land in an area between the Sine and the Gambia. Each village is made up of several lineages; authority over the family group passes from maternal uncle to nephew. Subjugated by their neighbors, the Wolof, who had a state organization, the Serer nevertheless played an important part in the political history of Senegal. President Léopold Sédar Senghor is a Serer by birth.

SHI (spear). Zaïre. Several chiefdoms were established on the eastern shore of Lake Kivu by immigrant pastorialists who seem to have gained acceptance peacefully by means of economic strength alone. They set up divine monarchies similar to those of their neighbors, the Rundi and Rwanda. The king was invested anew each year in a religious ceremony. The Shi are related to the Fulero who were involved in the armed rebellion against the central government of Léopoldville (now Kinshasa, in Zaïre) in 1964.

SHILLUK (spear). Sudan. 110,000. Living in the marshy area of the Upper Nile valley, these warrior pastoralists recognize the authority of their first king, Nyikang, and his descendants. His present successor resides permanently at Fashoda, but traditionally there was no fixed capital. The king, believed to be of divine origin, is associated with the mythical introducer of stock-raising. Cattle are a cultural symbol, rather than being of economic value, and confer socially recognized dignity on their owner. Like the other Nilotic people—such as the Nuer and the Dinka—the Shilluk have little material culture (they go naked) and an art rich in verbal expression but poor in the plastic arts.

SHONA (spear and granaries). Mozambique, Rhodesia. Over 1 million. This term refers to a group of agricultural peoples who herd cattle as a secondary activity. The Shona are believed to have set up a kingdom in the sixth century the sovereign of which, Monomotapa, held a brilliant court that impressed the first Portuguese explorers in the sixteenth century. Called the Karanga by the Portguese, this monarchy had the characteristics of a divine kingship. Another dynasty, the Rowzi, constructed certain buildings on the famous Zimbabwe site, a group of structures built of rough-cut granite blocks. As there are no other structures of this kind in the area, we cannot state with certainty which society built them, although it can no longer be doubted that they were built by Africans. The political and dynastic institutions of the Zimbabwe-Monomotapa are strikingly reminiscent of those of Ankole and Rwanda, according to certain anthropologists.

SOGA (spear). Uganda. 500,000. The Soga do not form a political unit. At the end of the nineteenth century, they were divided into about fifteen small kingdoms the dynasties of which regarded themselves either as descendants of the Bito or as the original inhabitants of the area. Anthropologists have stressed the importance of appointed officials in these Soga "Bantu bureaucracies." Conflicts over the royal succession were such that during a king's lifetime those who might succeed him were potential usurpers. Thus only men of non-royal descent, who could not claim the succession, were reliable servants of the king.

SONGE (granaries). Zaïre. Living in the wooded savannas of the Upper Lomami, the Songe have succeeded in preserving their autonomy during the major political realignments of the eighteenth and nineteenth centuries. They are culturally close to the Luba, the large society to the south. Their art is characteristically angular and aggressive. The sculptor often inserts magical substances into the statuettes. The carved masks give a powerful impression of strength; most are decorated with parallel grooves, which follow and emphasize the relief.

SONGHAI (cities). Mali, Upper Volta, Dahomey, Niger, Nigeria. 650,000. The Songhai grow rice, with millet as a secondary food. From the eleventh century on, Gao was the capital of a large empire that in the fifteenth century took advantage of the decline of the Malinke Empire but was itself checked by the expansion of Mali in the eighteenth century. The hegemony of the Songhai in the Western Sudan was thus maintained throughout the medieval period in Europe. Some princes converted to Islam. Today the Songhai are scattered throughout the Niger Valley, but as a legacy from their past they retain a stratified social structure in which classes and castes are still the basis of society. Craftsmanship is still flourishing.

SOTHO or BASUTO (spear). Lesotho, Botswana, South Africa. 1,400,000. The Tswana may be considered a branch of the Sotho; it was they who occupied what is now Botswana. 800,000 Sotho live in Lesotho, 130,000 of them working for periods in the mines of South Africa; and this has been an important factor in the political awakening of this old British enclave inside South Africa, which was given a constitution in 1959. The arid territory of Botswana has 350,000 inhabitants, only about 1 per square mile, but 400,000 Tswana live in the north of Cape Province and in the Transvaal.

SUK or PAKOT (spear). Kenya. 60,000. The Suk are Nilotic pastoralists and cultivators of sorghum; their social organization is similar to that of the Nuer. Their material culture is very simple. They have no true villages but only political units based on neighborhoods; differences between these are settled peacefully by recourse to certain religious chiefs. Experts in magic and divination, they are the only people with any power to exercise social control in these "acephalous" Nilotic societies.

SWAHILI (cities). Tanzania, Kenya. One million. Although they live far from the Sudan region, we class the Swahili in the civilization of cities because they manifest the main characteristics of that civilization. This term, which is of Arabic origin (*sahil*= coast; plural *sawahil*), designates the descendants of Muslim navigators who, from the eighth century on, set up commercial establishments all along the east coast of Africa, as far south as Mozambique. The influence of the Swahili language on the populations with which the Swahili interbred was such that *Kiswahili*, a Bantu language with many Arabic elements, is now spoken throughout East Africa from Somalia to Mozambique and in the interior beyond the Great Lakes in Eastern Zaïre. This language, in its pidgin form as a commercial language, is now, along with Fulani, the most important lingua franca of black Africa.

SWAZI (granaries). Swaziland. 180,000. The Swazi kingdom, probably founded at the end of the sixteenth century, absorbed the Ngoni, the Sotho and the Tonga, who, however, retained their own particular cultural characteristics. Their political system was very subtle. Although in principle the king was the supreme power, in actuality he was controlled by a complex hierarchy of officials more concerned with the permanence of the monarchy than with any particular dynasty. At the end of the nineteenth century the king was tricked into ceding half his territory to white settlers. This "paper conquest" gave rise to many disputes. Finally the kingdom was no longer recognized as an independent state. Although it was neutral in the Boer War (1899), the Swazi land was conquered by British troops and became the Swaziland Protectorate (1906). It remained a British enclave within the Republic of South Africa until 1968, when it became a kingdom under King Sobhuza II, who had been *Ingwenyama* (paramount chief) since 1921. At present, it has a population that includes 9000 white; its main products are asbestos and timber. Having very close economic ties with South Africa, Swaziland is in a delicate political situation, since the Republic of South Africa does not like this adjacent "island" in which its racist laws cannot be imposed.

TEKE (granaries). Congo-Brazzaville, Zaïre. 75,000. The Teke grow small grains and manioc. They are organized into chiefdoms in the highlands west of Brazzaville. Their chiefdoms united to form a strong kingdom that managed to free itself from the tutelage of the Loango. The people are very attached to their traditions, and they still participate to only a small degree in the political life of Congo where most of them live. They have a close relationship with the Binga populations at the edge of the forest belt. Their rough, massive sculpture is less finished than that of the Kongo. In certain modern works the face, expressive but simply carved, hardly stands out from the original block of wood. Faces are often elongated by a beard and show the traditional tattoo marks. Statuettes are made at the birth of a child to protect it and are discarded at puberty.

TETELA (clearings). Zaïre. 300,000. Also known by the name of *Hamba*, they belong to the Mongo group. They live in the Congo basin at the edge of the equatorial forest, between the Sankuru and Lomami rivers. Their material culture and way of life show their relationship to forest peoples. Patrice Lumumba came from a Tetela village.

THONGA (spear). Mozambique. Over 1 million. With these cattle herders, who do not entrust the care of cattle to women, agriculture plays an important economic role: cereals are the basic food, but root crops are a necessary supplement. The scattered villages are surrounded by a fence, inside which are the circular huts; a space is reserved for livestock. Within this large cultural group, various alliances resulted in the formation of small states, at the head of which the hereditary chiefs exercised powers almost as great as those of sacred kings.

TIV (granaries). Nigeria. 800,000. In the savannas south of the Benue, the Tiv are organized into chiefdoms of various sizes. Despite the absence of centralized political institutions, the Tiv have a feeling of identity as a people. This was especially evident just before Nigeria's independence, when the Tiv organized a serious uprising against the administrative authorities.

TORO (spear). Uganda. 150,000. Until 1830 the Toro were part of Bunyoro. The Ruwenzori mountains, the famous Mountains of the Moon, the highest peak reaching almost 15,600 feet, are in Toro country. The split off in the nineteenth century occurred in a manner quite common in such kingdoms: a son of the Nyoro king left the capital in secret, taking some royal herds with him. He settled in eastern Toro, where the local population was tired of being governed by the distant Bunyoro. A punitive expedition failed to subjugate the rebel son, and finally the king of the Nyoro accepted the fait accompli and sent his son a drum, symbol of royal power. The social and political organization of the Toro is, of course, very similar to that of the Bunyoro.

TUKULOR or TOUCOULEUR (cities). Senegal, Mali. 300,000. In the nineteenth century this Sudan people had its period of glory under the leadership of El-Hadj Omar, who was born in 1797 at Aloar, near Podor. He came from a Muslim family and went to Mecca, where he received the title of Khalif of the Sudan. On his return he settled in the Futa Djalon and proclaimed a holy war against the infidels. After subjugating the Malinke and the Bambara, he laid siege to Medina in 1857; the garrison had to be rescued by Faidherbe, leader of several French military expeditions in West Africa and founder of the colony of Senegal. Before his death in 1864, El-Hadj Omar seized Macina but failed to subjugate the Fulani, who continued to fight. His empire did not survive him.

TWA (bow and clearings). Zaïre, Rwanda, Burundi. This name is applied to groups that are now distinct, although they have a common origin. In the central basin of Zaïre, the Twa, numbering about 100,000, are Pygmies who have adopted a sedentary life and interbred with the Mongo. Although under Mongo influence the Twa became small-scale agriculturalists, they depend on the forest for most of their food; they are closely bound to the forest by their religious traditions. In Rwanda and Burundi the Twa constitute the Pygmy lower caste; they do not, however, form any considerable proportion of the population, there being less than 20,000 of them. Most of the Twa live in direct dependence on the Tutsi nobles, for whom they perform useful menial services; a minority still carry on the traditional way of life of hunters in the high forests of the Congo-Nile watershed.

WOLOF (cities). Senegal. 850,000. The Wolof are agriculturalists, politically organized into a kingdom; they dominated several tributary states the sovereigns of which recognized the authority of the Wolof *bur*. The Serer were among the societies subjected to Wolof authority. Kinship is reckoned matrilineally.

YAKA (granaries). Zaïre, Gabon. 7,300. These farmers, organized by chiefdoms, live in the Kwango area. In the art of wood sculpture, they are famous for their characteristic masks: a greatly exaggerated turned-up nose, and a hairdo in the form of a sort of flattened helmet.

YAO (granaries) Malawi, Mozambique, Tanzania. These cultivators of millet, manioc and maize are especially noteworthy for their family organization. The relationship between a man and his sister's son, important throughout Black Africa, is a very special bond among the Yao, being the basis of the social organization of the village. In their matrimonial system marriage is uxorilocal, that is, the husband goes to live with his wife's parents. The children of the marriage belong to their mother's lineage, and their mother's oldest brother has authority over them. There are also villages made up of the households of several sisters, in which the husbands are little more than visitors. But such an extreme situation is not found everywhere: a husband who is a wealthy chief can make his wife live with him. He then tends to transmit his authority to his eldest son and withholds from his rightful heirs, his sister's sons, part of their inheritance, to the advantage of his own son. This practice shows clearly the tensions inherent in a strictly matrilineal system.

YEKE (granaries). Zaïre. The Yeke live in a chiefdom founded in the middle of the nineteenth century not far from colonial Jadot-ville, by a Sumbwa, the son of an ivory dealer. Appointed by his father to be head of a caravan strongly armed with muskets bought from Arab traders, he took advantage of dissensions between local chiefs to have himself proclaimed king under the name of Msiri. He set up his capital at Bunkeya, which became a settlement of 15,000 inhabitants. Continuing to trade with Arabs who had settled in the Tanganyika area, he was able to maintain an army and so subjugate the neighboring chiefdoms. At their head he placed a representative, sometimes a woman, whose duty was to collect tribute. He was killed in 1891 in a battle with the troops of the Congo Free State. Msiri's kingdom lost some of its territory, but survived. Godefroid Munongo, who played a very important part in the secession of Katanga, is a Yeke and a descendent of Msiri.

YORUBA (cities). Nigeria (3 million) Dahomey (180,000). The language of the Yoruba is spoken by nearly five million people. These savanna agriculturalists lived in the nineteenth century in large towns (Ibadan, Iwo, Ogbomosho) and built up a complex political organization. While recognizing the *Oni* of Ife as the supreme authority in religious matters and the *Alafin* of Oyo in political, each city governed itself. The economic basis of Yoruba society is varied: agriculture, stock-raising, hunting, occasional fishing, iron mining, crafts, long-distance trade. Wooden doors, pillars and house-posts; divination cups; drums; staffs decorated with anthropomorphic motifs; all give some idea of the variety of work produced by wood sculptors, whose works are used in various cults. The Ife ceramics are known all over the world. Today the Yoruba have an important political position in the Western Province of Nigeria, of which Ibadan is the capital.

ZANDE (clearings and cities). Zaïre, Central African Republic, Sudan. 750,000. From south to north, Zande territory gradually changes from equatorial forest to savanna. The Zande, however, are forest people rather than savanna agriculturalists. The tsetse fly precludes stock-raising. Unlike the other peoples of the clearings—whom they resemble in that secret associations are very important in their culture—the Zande built up a monarchical-type state with the support of a nobility that supplied the district chiefs. Although the society as a whole recognized patrilineal descent, the ruling families gave preference to the maternal line. Since the eighteenth century, Islam has modified the social structures of this society.

ZINZA (spear). Tanzania. On the south shores of Lake Victoria, the Zinza kingdoms seem never to have known stability. When Speke crossed the area in 1861, the political units were in a constant state of division and realignment. At the end of the century the Germans settled in the area, and in World War I the Zinza suffered more than other groups from the recruitment of porters for the German troops. Finally in 1930 to 1935, epidemics of human sleeping sickness brought about population movements to tsetse-free areas. As a result of these various disasters, traditional Zinza structures are almost extinct, and knowledge of their past form is difficult to obtain.

ZULU (spear). South Africa. Three million. These cattle raisers also practice agriculture. A warrior people, they found in Chaka at the beginning of the nineteenth century a brilliant military leader who succeeded in bringing various groups under his authority, established control over broad territories and played a crucial part in the history of Southeast Africa. The wars, massacres and migrations caused by Chaka brought about realignments and schisms of peoples that completely changed the ethnic map of this part of Africa. Paradoxically, this warrior people destined by its size to play an important part in the struggle of the Africans of South Africa for emancipation, had as its spokesman the advocate of nonviolence Albert Luthuli who was awarded the Nobel Peace Prize in 1961.

BIBLIOGRAPHY

Books dealing with Black Africa as a whole from the cultural or social viewpoint are few in number if they are to fit the requirements that they be up to date, easily obtainable and written in English by specialists for non-specialists. The books listed here meet all these requirements.

GENERAL

Bohannan, Paul: *Africa and Africans*, Natural History Press, New York, 1964.

Davidson, Basil: *Africa in History*, Macmillan, New York, 1968.

Forde, Daryll (ed): *African Worlds. Studies in the Cosmological Ideas and Social Values of African Peoples*, Oxford University Press, London, 1965.

Herskovits, Melville J.: *The Human Factor in Changing Africa*, Alfred A. Knopf, New York, 1962.

Maquet, Jacques: *Civilizations of Black Africa*, Oxford University Press, New York, 1972.

Oliver, Roland, and Fage, John D.: *A Short History of Africa*, Penguin Books, Baltimore, 1962.

ART

Elisofon, Eliot, and Fagg, William: *The Sculpture of Africa*, Praeger, New York, 1958.

Laude, Jean: *The Arts of Black Africa,* University of California Press, Berkeley, California, 1971.

Leiris, Michel, and Delange, Jacqueline: *African Art,* Golden Press, New York, 1968.

Segy, Ladislas: *African Sculpture Speaks,* International University Booksellers, New York, 1969.

THE MODERN PERIOD

Mazrui, Ali A., and Rotberg, Robert I. (eds): *The Traditions of Protest in Black Africa, 1886–1966,* Harvard University Press, Cambridge, 1970.

Middleton, John (ed.): *Black Africa. Its Peoples and Their Cultures Today,* Macmillan, New York, 1970.

TRANSITIONAL SOCIETIES

Balandier, Georges: *Ambiguous Africa,* Meridian Books, New York, 1966.

Cohen, Ronald, and Middleton, John (eds.): *From Tribe to Nation in Africa,* Chandler, San Francisco, 1970.

Van Den Berghe, Pierre L.: *Africa. Social Problems of Change and Conflict,* Chandler, San Francisco, 1965.

The reader who wishes to learn more about various traditional societies will find many excellent monographs. Of course he will not always find one dealing with the particular society about which he wants more detailed information. But if he takes as a starting point a certain geographical area or one of the five civilizations, he is sure to find several recent books dealing with the societies of that area or civilization. The most useful method of finding these books is to consult, first, the bibliographies at the ends of the 55 chapters of *Africa. Its Peoples and Their Culture History* by George Peter Murdock (McGraw-Hill, New York, 1959). Then it is recommended to consult the series of volumes published by the International African Institute (London) under the general title *Ethnographic Survey of Africa,* edited by Professor Daryll Forde. This series now comprises more than 60 volumes. Each volume provides, arranged under the same headings, a summary of what is known about "a people or a group of related peoples" and a very full biblography in which it is easy to look up the best and most recent monographs. For modern Africa, an excellent bibliography is to be found in *The African Experience. Volume IIIA: Bibliography* edited by John N. Paden and Edward W. Soja (Northwestern University Press, Evanston, Ill., 1970).

INDEX